CONTENTS

SILENT CRIES *of a* STRONG WOMAN

Heal Her to Heal Me

MEKA SMITH, M.A., BSN, RN, RRT

FOREWORD MIN. CHRISTINE DOTSON

Silent Cries of a Strong Woman: Heal Her to Heal Me
Copyright © 2025 Meka Smith. All Rights Reserved.

No part of this book may be reproduced, stored in a retrieved system, or transmitted in any form or by any means — electronic, mechanical, photocopying, recording, scanning, or otherwise — without the prior written permission of the author.

Published in Little Rock, Arkansas, by ISpeak Publishing Service Little Rock, AR. Contact information: 501-519-6996 or Ispeakpublishing@gmail.com.

To order wholesale or bulk orders of this book, please contact the author directly at mekasmith22@yahoo.com.

Meka Smith is available for keynote addresses, workshops, panel discussions, consultations, and radio & television interviews by emailing mekasmith22@yahoo.com.

Printed in the United States of America
ISBN 979-8-218-86522-1

DEDICATION

To my Lord and Savior, Jesus Christ — without You, I am nothing. Thank You for redeeming my life from the ashes, for reaching into the depths of my brokenness, and breathing purpose into my pain. You took what was shattered and made it whole. Your turned silent cries into a victorious song of freedom, and grace.

To my husband, Pastor Tennyson B. Smith II — thank you for loving me with the heart of Christ, for covering me in prayer, and for standing by my side with unwavering faith and strength. You are God's tangible expression of love in my life, and I am forever grateful.

And to my abundant blessings, Imari, Isaiah, and Mia — you are my answered prayers and my greatest gifts from God. May your lives always reflect His glory, and may you know that every sacrifice was made so you could walk boldly in your divine purpose.

All glory to God, who makes all things beautiful in His time.

ACKNOWLEDGMENTS

First and foremost, I give glory and honor to my Heavenly Father, who has carried me through every valley and set me upon every mountain. Without His grace, none of this would be possible.

A special acknowledgment to my aunt, Minister Emma Winningham. You have walked this journey with me and poured into me my entire life. Your prayers, wisdom, and unconditional love have anchored me in ways words cannot fully express. I love you to the moon!

To the Brewer family — your love is God's hands at work in my life. You saw me through His eyes, nurtured me with His heart, and helped shape the woman He called me to be. I am forever grateful for the divine covering you have been—there is no me without you.

To Minister Christine Dotson, my sister and best friend for over 30 years. Thank you for loving me at my lowest, for never judging me, and for always celebrating my wins like they were your own. Your friendship is one of my life's greatest gifts.

To Rhonda, Ta'Vonna, Ronald, and Arthur, LaVell, Greg, Breyonte' & Devante— my beloved siblings. You all have been such a big part of my why. Being your big sis is one of my highest honors. I love y'all so much!

Last but certainly not least, I would like to thank my editor, Helaine R. Williams of Make it Plain Ministries, and my publisher, Tiffany S. Greene of ISpeak Publishing, for their diligent work.

To every mentor, friend, and intercessor who has prayed me through, encouraged me, and believed in the God within me — thank you. May this work bring Him glory and be a testament to the power of His redemptive love.

AUTHOR'S NOTE

Dear Reader,

I never knew how this book would come together. In fact, I spent most of my life hiding these silent cries, determined to appear strong, capable, and unbothered by the storms that shaped me. But God has a way of taking the places we tried to bury and using them to breathe life into others.

This book is not just a collection of my memories; it is a testament to God's redemptive love, His healing power, and His unwavering promise to make beauty from ashes. As you read these pages, I pray you find yourself in the stories, the reflections, and the raw truths. I pray you hear God whispering to your broken places, "Daughter, I see you. I have always seen you. And I will heal you."

My journey to healing is still unfolding, but I am no longer silenced by shame, fear, or insecurity. I am learning to walk in wholeness and freedom, and it is my deepest desire that you do too.

May these words be a mirror reflecting both the pain and the promise — and a lantern guiding you into your own freedom. Thank you for allowing me to share my heart with you.

With love and purpose,
Min. Meka Smith

FOREWORD

I met Meka over thirty years ago in high school. I can't recall exactly how our friendship began, but I do remember that we bonded over one thing — we didn't trust other females. At the time, we never talked about why, but looking back, I realize we were both moving through life with unhealed wounds and unspoken trauma. Neither of us could have imagined then that God would one day use our pain as a platform for healing — not only for ourselves, but for others.

Over the years, I have watched Meka rise from battles that would have broken many. She is a fighter — strong, determined, and relentless until the work is done. Her heart for people and her genuine compassion for those who are hurting reflect the love of Christ that has transformed her life. I've seen her walk through challenges with grace, faith, and perseverance, always giving God the glory.

Meka embodies strength, resilience, and authenticity. She is an amazing wife, mother, sister, friend, and leader whose life mirrors God's redemptive power. The wisdom she shares in Silent Cries of a Strong Woman comes from real-life experience and deep spiritual insight. Her prayers, affirmations, and reflections are both practical and biblically grounded — guiding readers to face their pain, embrace healing, and walk boldly into wholeness.

Healing requires courage. It means confronting what hurt you so you can reclaim your voice, your joy, and your power. This book is a tool for that journey — a call to do the hard work that leads to lasting freedom.

I wholeheartedly endorse "Silent Cries of a Strong Woman" and the transformative message it carries. It will bless your life as it has blessed mine.

With love and honor,
Minister Christine Dotson

TESTIMONIAL

This book is not just a memoir — it is a mirror for every woman who has ever looked flawless on the outside but carried invisible wounds on the inside. With raw honesty, grace, and unflinching courage, Meka Smith peels back the layers of her life, inviting us into the deeply personal journey of a little girl who grew up behind masks — masks of strength, success, and perfection.

From the painful realities of domestic violence, emotional neglect, and generational trauma, to the internal war between who she appeared to be and who she truly was, she reminds us that survival is not healing, and appearances are not peace. Her words, anchored in Scripture, reflect a God who not only sees but sets us apart — even when our world says we are not enough. In an era where transparency is "avoided," the author understands that her journey was designed to help others fulfill their destiny.

As you turn these pages, be prepared to confront your own masks, your hidden wounds, and the lies trauma taught you. This story does not glorify pain, but it honors the process of becoming whole. It calls out the dysfunction that shaped so many of us and boldly declares that it stops here — with truth, with healing, with God. Whether you're a woman who grew up too fast, a mother breaking generational curses, or simply someone ready to meet your true self, this book is for you. It's Meka's desire that the little girl who once felt forgotten, unseen, and unloved has a voice now — and she's telling her story, not just for herself, but for all of us.

It's an honor to recommend "Silent Cries of a Strong Woman" not only to this generation, but to generations to come. Your voice is valuable, and it must be heard.

Apostle Barbara J. McClain
San Antonio, Texas

INTRODUCTION

For as long as I can remember, I've been the strong one. The dependable one. The one everyone runs to for advice, prayer, support, or a listening ear. I've worn the mask well — the mask of success, of unbreakable faith, of resilience, of poise. On the outside, my life looked picture-perfect: a thriving career, a beautiful home, an incredible husband, amazing children, and influence that many only dream of. But beneath it all were silent cries that no one ever heard. Cries for healing. Cries for freedom. Cries for someone to see me beyond my titles, my gifts, my beauty, and my accomplishments.

This book is my journey of peeling back every layer of pain, trauma, and silent suffering that I carried for decades. It is the raw, unfiltered truth of how childhood trauma shaped my identity, my decisions, my relationships, and even how I saw God. It is the story of a woman who learned that true healing could not come by ignoring the cries of the little girl within her. I had to go back and rescue her, love her, validate her, and speak life over her wounds so that Adult Me could finally breathe.

"Silent Cries of a Strong Woman: Heal Her to Heal Me" is not just my story — it's yours too. It is the story of every woman who has ever smiled through tears, served while secretly broken, or loved others while silently loathing herself. It is for the woman who is tired of being everything to everyone and nothing to herself. It is for the woman who knows God has called her higher but feels chained by the trauma of her past.

Through these pages, you will find hope, validation, strategy, truth, and the unshakable reality of God's redemptive love. You will confront your own silent cries and finally hear God whisper, "Daughter, you are seen. You are chosen. You are free."

My prayer is that this book becomes the oxygen mask your soul has been gasping for so that you can walk in your healing, own your story, and become the unstoppable force of purpose and freedom you were always created to be.

CHAPTER 1

The Girl Behind the Mask

Scripture Focus: Jeremiah 1:5 (NIV)

Before I formed you in the womb I knew you, before you were born, I set you apart … .

Even before the pain, the rejection, the abuse, and the fear, God knew you. He saw you, and He set you apart. Trauma lied to you, but God's truth never changed.

From the outside looking in, you would think I had it all together. Hair always on point. My outfit matching my stilettos. Nails done. Toes done. Makeup on point.

I walk with confidence, my head held high. I have a wonderful husband and three amazing children. We live in a beautiful home in a middle-class Texas neighborhood. I drive a luxury vehicle. I hold two undergraduate degrees and a master's degree. I am a nurse by trade, but I run my own business. I have more freedom and flexibility than I've ever had in my life where my career is concerned. I am a Pastor's wife and a Pastoral Counselor. I travel. I love a great night out with my girls. I take great vacations with my husband and with our family. I can pretty much come and go as I please. I'm approaching 50 and let's just say, Father Time has been good to me. My "face card" is not declining.

So why am I still hurting?

Everything looks like I have it going on, but there are broken pieces of me that only God Himself can put back together. I hide behind the mask of having it all together because that's what I've been taught to do. I've got the respect and the prestige, but I have felt dead inside for so long. The inside definitely has not matched the outside.

So today, I begin to take off the mask, peel back the layers, and expose my vulnerability and the disconnect between who I really am underneath, and how I show up to this world.

From the moment I learned that the world was not safe, I learned to hide behind smiles, achievements, and my own strength. I wore masks that concealed the pain, trauma, abandonment, abuse, and disappointment. I was so good with the masks that I had long forgotten the little girl who was buried underneath all the rubbish longing for the opportunity to breathe through all that was suffocating her.

I was born to a teenage mother and an incarcerated father in the Midwest city of Gary, Ind. (aka Steel City) — a place known as the murder capital of the world for most of my childhood. From the very beginning, life felt heavy. As the oldest of nine children, I carried a responsibility I couldn't name and a loneliness I couldn't explain.

I was a beautiful brown girl with long ponytails, and even as a little one, I carried a presence about me. If talking were a sport, I would have won many gold medals! I loved people! People were drawn to me — they always have been. But inside, I just wanted what every little girl wanted: to be loved, to be accepted, and to feel safe. Those three things, the things I wanted most, always seemed to escape me.

I loved the fun times with my cousins. They were like my sisters. We would play for hours, laughing, pretending, creating worlds away from the one we were stuck in. My favorite toy was my Cabbage Patch doll, Mindy. She was my partner, my comfort. I would play with her, creating stories where I was the loved little girl and she was my best friend who never left. I also used my beloved doll baby to re-enact the realities of the abuse I saw occur between my mom and stepfather. Once, while sitting at the edge of the bathtub in our apartment, I took Betadine and poured it down my leg. I picked Mindy up, held her close to me and said, "Look at what your daddy did to me!" I was acting out what I'd seen.

Domestic violence was like a monster that crept through the walls of my childhood home, shaking everything in its path. I remember lying in my bed at night, covers pulled tightly to my chin, trembling with fear as I heard the yelling and the breaking of glass. My little body would shake so hard that my teeth would chatter. I felt so alone and helpless, terrified that at any given moment the violence would spill over into my room. The feeling of powerlessness seeped deep into my bones and into my soul, leaving me with a haunting fear that would linger in my life for many years after the shouting had stopped.

My father … Oh how I longed for him. I was a daddy-less daughter who only saw her father inside prison walls for as long as I could remember. His absence left a hole that no one else could fill. I had no understanding of what it meant to have a dad. I was 12 by the time my dad was released from prison. I remember being excited, yet so afraid. I had already been molested and knew that many of my sister-cousins had experienced the same.

From an early age I had to fend for myself. Survival wasn't a concept I learned later in life; it was a daily reality as a child. My siblings, my cousins and I were often dropped off at our Grannie's house while our mothers were all doing God knows what. We were left in the care of a schizophrenic aunt who talked to herself and was incapable of truly watching over us. There were no rules, no structure, and no real safety net. Just a pack of hot dogs, a can of pork 'n beans, a loaf of bread, and a house full of cousins trying to make sense of chaos. We got into anything and everything we could think of because no one was there to stop us.

What felt like freedom as a child was actually neglect wrapped in survival. It was in those early, unsupervised days that the mask began to form: one that said, "I'm fine," while deep down I was already learning that I had to protect myself while caring for others, and find belonging in broken places.

At home, I never saw an example of a healthy marriage. My mother chose men over her children repeatedly. It was confusing and painful to watch. She brought various men around us when my stepdad was away. I saw her have sex with these men. My mother was not a faithful wife at all! I didn't really understand what I was looking at, but I knew it wasn't right. I knew even as a young girl that the way she moved made me feel very uncomfortable. Her choices would eventually call into question the paternity of my siblings. I always knew who *my* father was, but my siblings, unbeknownst to them, grew up under a dark cloud of paternity uncertainty. Seeing my mother with different men left me feeling unsafe, unprotected, and confused about love, commitment, and family.

I struggled to keep friends because my mother moved us around the city so much. We often found ourselves having to become accustomed to new neighborhoods, new schools, and new faces ... and, sometimes, some strange places. I always felt like an outsider looking in. I longed for my mother's love, but she never seemed able to give it. Instead, I was exposed far too early to adult things — molestation, domestic violence, and pain that left me feeling dirty, broken, and small. I often felt like a stranger in my own home, especially after my siblings came along.

A defining moment in my childhood came when I was just seven years old. My mother had a mental breakdown right in front of me. The strong, gorgeous, fun-loving, proud woman I knew cracked before my eyes. The memories of that day will forever be etched on my brain. I was alone with my mom, scared and unsure what to do. Her episode went on for hours, and she was never the same again. I was never the same. (Her mental decline worsened as I grew older.)

After that, fear became a constant companion. I learned early on that adults could not be trusted to protect or nurture me. I had no framework for what a father's affirmation looked like, and a healthy mother-daughter relationship was not a part of my daily life. God was distant, seated somewhere far off in heaven, detached from my reality. He felt like every other adult in my life: unreachable, unavailable, and not coming to rescue me. What I didn't know then, but would later come to understand, is that an orphan spirit had already taken root in me. I was a daughter in need of covering, love, and protection, but I had no one in position to offer it. And deep down, I began to believe I wasn't worthy of it.

Behind my pretty smile and long ponytails was a little girl wearing an invisible mask — hiding her fear, her loneliness, and her silent cries for love.

REFLECTION QUESTIONS

1. What do you remember most about yourself as a child?
2. What did you long for most as a child?
3. What mask did you wear to hide your pain or fear?
4. Where did you feel the safest growing up?
5. What example of love and family did you see growing up, and how did it shape your beliefs?

PRAYER

Father, thank You that before I was ever formed in my mother's womb, You knew me. You saw me even when I felt invisible. You set me apart even when I felt discarded. Heal the little girl in me who wore a mask to survive. Reveal to me the truth of who I am in You — loved, seen, chosen, and never forgotten. In Jesus' name, Amen.

DECLARATION

I am seen by God. He knew me before I was formed. I am not forgotten. I am chosen and deeply loved.

The girl behind the mask learned to smile through silent pain, pretending to be whole while breaking inside. But the mask didn't form on its own—it was shaped by the harsh words and heavy hands that bruised her spirit and silenced her voice.

MY SILENT REFLECTIONS

CHAPTER 2

Bruised by Her Words, Broken by Her Hands

Scripture Focus: Proverbs 18:21 (NIV)

The tongue has the power of life and death, and those who love it will eat its fruit.

Her words spoke death over me, but God's Word speaks life to resurrect who He created me to be.

Her words didn't just sting — they scarred. I remember moments when her tongue felt sharper than any belt or slap. "You'll never be nothing," she'd say. Or, "You're just like your daddy," as if it were a curse. Those statements took root in the soil of my young heart and grew into weeds of insecurity, self-doubt, and shame. Long before I understood my identity in Christ, I was labeled by someone who was supposed to nurture me — and those false labels became a lens through which I saw myself for years.

The physical pain came and went, but the emotional bruises? They lingered. She didn't need to raise her hand every time — the emotional distance, the looks of disgust, the ignoring of my pleas, and the inconsistency in her love told me everything I needed to know. I started to believe that love looked like instability, volatility, and fear. I didn't have the language then, but I lived in survival mode, constantly wondering what version of her I'd wake up to. Her hands weren't hands that healed; they hurt, and they haunted me for a long time.

There were moments when the violence turned terrifying — when the rage in her eyes looked like she didn't see me as her daughter anymore. I got spankings as a child for the normal things kids get spanked for. But when I turned 14 — the same age she was when she got pregnant with me — something shifted. She started physically attacking me. The older I got, the more she would fight me like I was another grown woman. When we had disagreements, she would lose control. One day, she got so upset with me that she grabbed me by my hair, threw me to the ground, and stomped me. Each blow left a scar on my soul. The emotional abuse and neglect she inflicted left scars far greater than any physical abuse ever could. God did not let her kill me — not physically, and not spiritually. Even when I didn't know how to call on Him, He was already covering me. Isaiah 54:17 (NKJV) says, "No weapon formed against you shall prosper," and I am living proof of that promise.

There's a unique kind of devastation that comes from believing your own mother hates you. It's not just painful — it's identity-shattering. A mother is supposed to be your first safe place, the one who nurtures and protects. Instead, I became the target of her bitterness, the punching bag for her unhealed wounds. Her eyes looked through me with resentment. Her words landed like knives. And in my young mind, I didn't know how to separate her rage from my worth. I thought I deserved it. I thought something was wrong with me. That kind of rejection doesn't just bruise — it brands. And it took years of God's tender love, prayer, and *unlearning* to finally understand that her hatred was never about who I was — it was about who she never healed to become.

Surprisingly enough, I had once felt very close to my mom. She was once my whole world. I wanted to be with her at every moment, to sit up under her and just belong to her. She completed her associate's degree in business. I saw her walk across the stage in her white cap and gown. I was so proud of her. It was such a huge accomplishment. I used to go to work with her. She was a secretary who could type what seemed like a thousand words a minute. Did I mention how beautiful she was? She had the most beautiful smooth, dark-chocolate skin that glowed, and pearly white teeth with a gorgeous smile. But it all changed so quickly. She turned into this cold-hearted, disconnected person that I no longer recognized.

Even when I tried to do everything right, it was never enough. I was either too much or not enough — too loud, too sensitive, too emotional. Yet I kept trying, kept striving, hoping that one day I might earn the tenderness I craved. But love isn't something a child should have to earn. That distortion made me chase approval in all the wrong places later in life — in friendships, in men, even in ministry. I didn't know it yet, but I was bleeding emotionally from wounds no one could see.

Even in those dark and confusing moments, God saw me. The same God revealed in Psalm 34:18 — "The Lord is close to the brokenhearted and saves those who are crushed in spirit" (NIV) — was drawing near, even when I couldn't feel Him. Every bruise, every harsh word — none of it escaped His notice. He was already planning my healing.

I used to watch my cousin Tesley with quiet envy. Her mom treated her like a treasure, laughing with her, hugging her for no reason, calling her by a nickname. It wasn't perfect, but it was safe. They always went places together. They shared secrets like best friends. I didn't know what that kind of warmth felt like. I'd sit in my room in silence, aching for a mother-daughter bond like theirs — a place where I could be soft without punishment, where I could be seen without criticism. I loved my cousin and my aunt, but that envy lived like a secret ache in my soul. It reminded me of what I longed for most: to feel chosen and cherished by the woman who gave me life.

Intentionally or not, my mother shaped who I became as a woman. I learned to do what I had to do for myself. Her abandonment, abuse, and neglect taught me how to survive, how to fight for myself, and how to push through pain like it was normal. From her, I learned how to keep moving even with a broken heart and how to wear strength like a badge of honor. But I also inherited emotional silence, mistrust, and the inability to receive help without guilt. Her version of womanhood was rooted in hardness and, for a long time, so was mine. It took time, healing, and God's relentless love for me to realize that my strength didn't have to come from suffering. I could be strong and soft, powerful and loved.

It wasn't until I had a true encounter with God's presence that the breakthrough began. I was in a moment of deep reflection, full of pain, when the Lord gently reminded me: "I saw it all, and I still chose you." That wrecked me. His love met me in the darkest places of my childhood and kept me. For the first time, I realized I wasn't what my mother said I was — I was who God said I was: loved, chosen, and deeply seen. That moment became a turning point. I no longer chased her approval or carried her hatred as my identity. I began to heal. I began to forgive. And I began to walk in this truth: God had been protecting, preserving, and calling me all along.

REFLECTION QUESTIONS

1. What are the words spoken over you by your mother and father that still echo in your heart today?
2. What was the difference between physical pain and emotional pain for you?
3. Where did you find small glimpses of safety and hope during that time?

4. How did your mother's and father's treatment shape the way you love and mother your own children today?
5. What mask did you wear to hide your pain from others?
6. What is one truth God is speaking today to replace the lies you were told?

PRAYER

Lord, heal the wounds from my mother's words and hands. Help me forgive her and release her brokenness to You. Help me to heal from the abandonment and rejection of my father. Replace every lie spoken over me with Your truth. Restore my identity as Your beloved daughter. Help me mother my children from a place of healing and wholeness. In Jesus' name, Amen.

DECLARATION

I declare today that I am not defined by the words that wounded me or the hands that harmed me. I am who God says I am — fearfully and wonderfully made. Every curse spoken over my life is broken in Jesus' name. I renounce every lie that told me I was worthless, unlovable, or undeserving of good things. I declare that I am loved deeply by my Heavenly Father. His words are life to me, and His hands are gentle and healing. Where I was bruised, He makes me whole. Where I was broken, He restores me. I walk in freedom from the pain of my past, and I rise today clothed in dignity, strength, and truth.

My mother's abuse and abandonment left a wound that would keep getting infected over and over again. Each no, each dismissal, each betrayal added another layer to my identity of rejection.

MY SILENT REFLECTIONS

CHAPTER 3

When Love Felt Like Rejection

Scripture Focus: Isaiah 53:3 (NIV)

He was despised and rejected by mankind, a man of suffering, and familiar with pain.

Jesus knows the sting of rejection and meets you there with His perfect acceptance.

Healthy parenting is the foundation of a child's emotional, psychological, and spiritual development. When children are raised in nurturing, loving, secure environments, they develop confidence, self-worth, and resilience that shape their entire lives. Research shows that children with supportive, engaged parents are more likely to excel academically, maintain strong mental health, and avoid risky behaviors (Child Trends, 2019). But when parenting is absent, inconsistent, abusive, or neglectful, the wounds run deep. Children who grow up without loving parental care often carry invisible scars of abandonment, rejection, and confusion, leading to long-term issues such as depression, anxiety, substance abuse, and unhealthy relationships.

In these moments of loss, God's Word offers comfort and truth: "When my father and my mother forsake me, then the Lord will take me up." (Psalm 27:10, KJV) Even when earthly parents fail, God steps in as our perfect Father, holding us close and calling us His own.

In the summer of 2008, while pregnant with my youngest son, I was sitting in the waiting room of the Gary Health Department. I had taken my mother there for a mental-health evaluation to get her additional services. I sat in a seat next to my father. My mother sat across the waiting room with my youngest sister. My husband had been unable to travel with me, and I did not go around my mother without my husband or my father present as my mother would attack me physically, even after I'd become an adult woman.

I looked back and forth from my mother to my father, wondering how they even got together. My mother is paranoid schizophrenic and has been most of my life. My dad was never abusive to me, but his abandonment and rejection of me when he went to prison, and then again when he came home, hurt just as bad as the pain my mother caused me. (I once told my dad, in a joking way, that the only difference between him and her is that she has an official diagnosis and he needed one. He didn't like that too much.)

I felt rejected from the time I was five years old. That was when my mother married my stepfather. It was the last time I felt seen and genuinely heard by her. Everything changed so quickly. Her attention was gone, and so was her tenderness.

At school, I was teased and rejected by friends. When I was in junior high school, I had to share toiletries with my mother. One day she sent me to school after refusing to provide me with any deodorant. I endured the traumatic experience of being made fun of for being musty. That was embarrassing and devastating!

We were poor, so I didn't have nice things. My mother dressed me in mature clothes — things she liked, not what little girls wore. I hated it. I was already insecure, and I felt awkward in my own skin. I spent a lot of time wishing I were somebody else.

I had no parents at school events or awards programs to cheer me on. I was rejected by my dad after he married his first wife. For the first few years after he was released from prison, my getting to spend one-on-one time with him on the weekends was the greatest time. I finally had my own dad — not my stepdad, but my own dad — to myself. When he got married, our visits were a flurry of excitement initially. But that excitement faded when he started to favor my stepbrother over me. And when he and his wife began having sons together, the rejection only deepened.

I grew up with my dad's absence as a scar on my soul. I had carried the shame of having an incarcerated father for most of my childhood. He had even told me to lie to my friends and tell them he was away at college. The lie felt safer than the truth, but it only added to the heartache. And when I finally got the chance to be with him in person, it ended in more heartache.

Every day felt like rejection. Everything had been stolen from me. My dad's rejection was the most hurtful. He was my last resort for the love I so desperately wanted from a parent. In his absence, his family showered me with the love I needed. They were my safe haven. But when my dad built his new family, I quickly took a backseat. Not only did I feel rejected, but seeing the way my dad doted on and favored his boys, I felt like I was a mistake.

The most earth-shattering rejection came from my mother when I graduated from high school. There had been an incident in which her latest boyfriend was inappropriate with me. My mother sided with him and refused to believe what I told her. I was no longer living at home at the time; I had been removed from her custody due to repeated abuse. But I still wanted my mom to come and see her firstborn daughter graduate. I still wanted her to be proud of me! I made sure that she had a ticket and transportation to my graduation.

But she was insistent on having her boyfriend there — a man who was not my father, nor her husband, but a monster! This monster is who tore up our family in the first place. This was the same man she had told *me* to stay away from after he touched me. She told me that if he couldn't come, she was not coming. That day, I made a declaration I had no idea would come true years later. I told her, "You chose a man over your own child. One day you're gonna look up, and you're not gonna have your children *or* him."

Needless to say, my mother was not there to see me graduate from high school. I remember standing there in my cap and gown, scanning the crowd for her face, hoping she had changed her mind — but she never showed up. My dad, stepmom, and a host of other family showed up for me, but there was still that emptiness that nothing could fill, the pain of knowing my own mother didn't think I was worth showing up for on one of the biggest days of my life.

My mom sent flowers to my aunt's house, but she could not use a bouquet of roses to make up for how she'd hurt and rejected me. I tried to trash the flowers, but my aunt wouldn't let me.

Because I didn't feel accepted by my parents, I learned to self-reject to save others the trouble. I learned that love was performance-based. I felt that if I performed well and made others happy, I'd get the love, acknowledgment, and acceptance I needed. I struggled with relationships my whole life because of rejection, insecurity, and low self-esteem. I struggled with accepting myself and expected others to do for me what I couldn't do for myself. Rejection became kryptonite; I needed the applause.

I didn't grow up going to church. I knew God existed, but I didn't think He saw me in any particular way. I didn't necessarily feel rejected by Him, but I didn't understand Him. I didn't know that there was a real plan and purpose for me. I simply felt like a mistake, unable to understand why the two people most responsible for me being here didn't want me.

REFLECTION QUESTIONS

1. What is your earliest memory of rejection, and how has it shaped your view of love?
2. Who did you long for acceptance from the most?
3. Where do you still feel rejection as an adult who God wants to heal?
4. What would you say to your younger self today about being enough?
5. How has God shown you that His love is not performance-based?

PRAYER

Lord, heal the wounds from my father's absence. Help me forgive him and release these broken pieces to You. Replace every lie spoken over me with Your truth. Restore my identity as Your beloved daughter.

DECLARATION

I declare that I am no longer defined by the absence of my earthly father. My identity, worth, and value come from my Heavenly Father who has always loved me, chosen me, and called me his own. I release every wound of rejection, abandonment, and neglect. I choose to stand firm in the truth that I am deeply loved, fully accepted, and forever secure in God. I declare that I am not fatherless. I am a daughter of the King, and his love completes me.

As I began to navigate carrying the wounds of a daddy-less daughter, I realized that his absence left more than just an empty chair at special moments. It created deep voids and unanswered questions that shaped my sense of self. But what I didn't fully understand at the time created dark spaces within me; dark spaces where secrets hid.

When you grow up feeling unseen, you learn how to hide. You learn to cover up your pain and keep your truth tucked away in silent corners. While my father's abandonment and mother's abuse are part of my story, it was the secrets I kept hidden in the shadows that nearly destroyed me.

MY SILENT REFLECTIONS

CHAPTER 4

Secrets in the Shadows

Scripture Focus: I Peter 5:10 (NIV)

And the God of all grace, who called you to his eternal glory in Christ, after you have suffered a little while, will himself restore you and make you strong, firm and steadfast.

He saw every secret pain in the shadows and remains close to you, binding your wounds with His perfect love.

The shadows of sexual trauma hide deep within a child's soul, but as that child grows into an adult, the hidden pain seeps into every area of life — stealing peace, distorting love, and leaving scars on the mind that only God's truth can heal.

I spent so much of my life scared of everything, not realizing how big a role early exposure to sexual images; molestation; and events happening to those close to me played in perpetuating that fear.

The earliest instance of inappropriate sexual exposure seemed to happen in a vacuum. One day while I was playing in the window at my stepdad's mom's house, my aunt's husband exposed his penis to me. I was crippled with fear and took off running, yelling back at him that I was going to tell. He yelled after me that I'd better not tell — so I didn't.

For two years following that incident, I was left alone on numerous occasions with a male cousin who was babysitting me. He started off playing the "tickle game" with me. There was lots of laughter the first few times it occurred. I realized only after quite some time that it was not a fun game anymore. I started to feel deeply uncomfortable, not realizing I was being molested and violated.

I later found that this sexual abuse was a generational curse. I had numerous cousins who were molested and fondled by various family members. I had aunts who had been violated by men my grandmother had brought around them. My mother confessed to me after I got married that she too had been violated, by someone my grandmother was involved with. Another uncle exposed himself to some of my cousins and me when we were young girls. My mother brought a man around my two sisters and me; he came after us too. When I left home for college, right under my mother's nose, that same monster sexually assaulted my sister and took her down such a dark path it almost stole her mind years later.

My mother, who was housesitting for one of her sisters during Christmas, was sternly warned not to have any of her lovers at her house. Now I was a nosy child; I watched and listened to everything. Within hours, my mother had one of her men in my aunt's bed, and I saw them having sex.

Even my grandmother was known to be involved with multiple men. Now don't get me wrong, Grannie was great to me. She provided a safe place to which I could run when my mom was being abusive. But one day, having been instructed by Grannie to stay put in a particular part of the house while she left for a bit, I eventually wandered off to the basement door. The door had no knob on it. I peeked through the hole, only to see her engaged in sexual activity with one of her tenants. A wave of horror hit me, leaving my little mind reeling, my thoughts tangled in fear and confusion that I didn't have words for.

From a young age, my cousins and I were exposed to a world filled with dysfunction, pathology, and perversion — an inheritance of brokenness we couldn't yet understand. Many of us share the painful testimony of being violated as young girls. My favorite cousin was violated, and in many ways, we were mirror girls, reflecting each other's innocence and pain. When my mom explained what had happened to my cousin, I felt sick to my stomach, unable to comprehend how someone could hurt her like that. The first time I saw my cousin after she returned from the hospital, words failed us. We just stood there for a few moments. Then we embraced, offering each other understanding, support, and a silent acknowledgment of our shared trauma.

A sickness permeated the moral fiber of my mom's family, a sickness that started with the grandparents. As we girls got older and things started to come out, we weren't met with love, understanding, care, or safety. We were met with, "It happened to all of us — get over it." This is exactly why mental illness has plagued the family. No one was willing to acknowledge and heal their own pain and trauma, so there was no space for them to help us face our own traumas.

Because of the lies I believed about myself and what I saw in the dynamic in which my mother operated, I was sold on finding a boy to love and give my all so that I could get what I needed in return. That led to promiscuity, a need to give myself away to be loved. I understood that sexual sin and secrecy went hand in hand. I thought it was my fault when I was violated. At least now, I thought, I could be in control of who I gave myself to.

The biggest thing that kept me from disclosing my sexual trauma to anyone, especially my mom, was the fear of her disbelief, her rejection, her flat-out blaming me. I didn't feel safe with her, nor did

I trust her. I was confused and felt devalued and unassured by the things I saw and experienced.

My trauma from my sexual abuse manifested as anxiety, fear, and perfectionism. I didn't trust men. I thought it was only a matter of time before a man would hurt me, just as various men had hurt my cousins and me. I ran from the pain of my trauma for many years. I thought if I got away from home, I would be free and healed, but then I realized that was just geography. I had a sack of issues I was carrying around with me. I learned to be controlling, to "take charge" of every situation to keep anyone from ever hurting me again. I learned to be all or none. I ran through life like a bull in a China shop, never slowing down to allow myself to *feel* or *experience*. I was in full-on denial.

REFLECTION QUESTIONS

1. What secrets have you carried in silence for too long?
2. How has this trauma affected your ability to trust and love yourself and others?
3. Where do you still need God's truth to heal hidden pain?
4. What is one step you can take today to continue your healing journey?

PRAYER

Father God, thank You for seeing the pain I carried in secret. Heal every wound left by sexual trauma and set me free from its power over my life. Replace every lie I believed about myself with Your truth. Help me to see myself as pure, loved, and worthy in Your eyes. In Jesus' name, Amen.

DECLARATION

I am not what happened to me. I am who God says I am — healed, loved, and whole!

As I reflect on the secrets in the shadows, I realize they were never meant to stay buried but hiding them became my survival. I carried those secrets with me into every place I lived, tucking them in deeper with each move, in each broken chapter forward. While the shadows held my secrets, the houses I lived in held my pain. They had four walls and a roof but no safety, no belonging, no true love to protect me.

And so, as we leave behind the secrets in the shadows, we now step into the reality of what it felt like to live in houses that were never really home.

MY SILENT REFLECTIONS

CHAPTER 5

Houses That Weren't Homes

Scripture Focus: Psalm 90:1 (NIV)

Lord, you have been our dwelling place throughout all generations.

True home is not found in bricks and wood but in the unchanging presence of God, who shelters, loves, and anchors us no matter where we lay our heads.

When I think of home, I think of safety, love, and warmth — a place where vulnerability is welcome and love is felt — but as a child, my everyday life left me feeling homeless.

I grew up bouncing between four different families. I had my mom and dad's families, and I also had the families of my stepdad and my stepmother. My mom moved us around our city so much that there was never a place to truly call home. We lived in apartments; my mom was never a homeowner. But even if we had owned a house, she would have had no idea how to make it a home. Time at home with my mom taught me that love hurts and that it was not freely given.

I tried to ignore that deep ache within, an ache that stemmed from the knowledge that my own mother could not stand me. When I was a child, she did not tell me she loved me. My mom rarely showed me tenderness or affection. Matter of fact, she never had a kind word to say to me. She resented me to the point that I felt that had I been on fire, she wouldn't even bother to spit on me.

Bouncing around between four families on any given weekend bred instability and added to my insecurity. I had no idea who I was, or who I was supposed to be, because of ever-changing people, places, things, and situations. I decided at a very young age that I had to protect myself. My safety was in my own hands, and nobody else was going to be able to hurt me.

I felt the safest and most grounded with my dad's family. They were amazing — God-fearing, loving, and fun. Their house was a small, cozy home, full of love, laughter, and great food. I am flooded with warm, fuzzy memories of my aunt preparing and serving my cousins and me delicious meals. I can hear the joy and laughter — that sense of togetherness and belonging. No matter how long the visits were or how much time passed in between, I always felt at home with them, welcomed by them. I knew they wanted me. I knew they loved me. I knew they *saw* me. If I didn't matter to anybody else in the world, I mattered to that family, and that was a huge anchor in my childhood. (That made it so much harder for me as I got older, especially when many of them began to move away after my grandmother passed and my Big Daddy remarried. My father lived over an hour away.)

In my everyday life with my mom, it was a totally different dynamic. The place in which we lived the longest was a white two-story apartment building. Just envisioning it reminds me of how cold, hard, and empty that place really was. We lived upstairs, and my mother's sister lived downstairs. I spent most of my years, through high school, there. That place is marked with some of the most traumatic memories of my childhood. Domestic violence and the toxicity of my mom and stepdad's marriage stained the walls. That building represented loneliness and isolation. It was the place where I lost my family because my mother and stepfather broke up and she moved in her boyfriend — the monster. That place represents nothing but pain, heartache, and the death of my innocence.

When we first moved there, my mother, stepdad, my two younger sisters and I lived there together. We spent a lot of time with cousins who would come over to hang out. But my mom's dynamic with her siblings was not great. They were not a close family. We often visited my grandmother's house, but she didn't have a true home either. There was a lot of pain and baggage, and my grandmother was not the type of matriarch who tried to bring her children together.

Among my most painful memories was of the day my mother pulled a gun on her own sister right in front of us. It began as a disagreement about phone messages. Then, a shoe was tossed back and forth. My baby sister got caught in the crossfire while in her carrier seat and she started screaming. Before I could blink, my mom and my aunt were tussling and throwing blows. Before I could get out of the way, I got hit. I retreated to Grannie's kitchen for safety. Moments later, my mother appeared in the hall doorway with Grannie's gun at her side. I was in shock! How could she fight, and then pull a gun on, her own sister? Grannie yelled for my mother to calm down and put her gun back where she got it.

These were not teenagers fighting over clothes or who stole who's boyfriend. These were grown women, one with a husband, and both had children. As my chin started throbbing, I started to see blood coming from my mouth. I checked inside my lip and saw that I was injured. In the midst of their melee, one of them had knocked a sizable hole in my gums!

For quite a while, life with my dad and stepmom was a welcome reprieve from mess like this. My stepmom's family would visit often, but they partied and drank a lot. My stepmom was twelve years younger than my dad, but eight years older than me — quite a pistol but mature for her age. She loved to party, but she was good to me. She poured into me and loved me like a daughter. She saw me, seemed to understand my pain, and did what she could to comfort me. She even made my dad pay more attention to me. She and my dad fought too. But I still felt it was better to be with them. My dad didn't really know how to be a dad, but I knew he loved me and tried to show it in his own way.

My dad and stepmom lived in an apartment until they bought their first home — a wonderful one-story house with a basement that my dad remodeled into a beautiful space for his family. We made some amazing memories there. Now, that was a home for me, but temporarily. It didn't belong to me; I only visited, during weekends and breaks. I had no home in my everyday life. But being with my dad was a temporary reprieve from my mom. Although not perfect, it was a way to get away from the chaos and toxicity.

One thing I could not escape was the domestic violence that echoed through the walls of my childhood dwellings. I could not escape the effects of alcoholism, which consumed both my stepdad and my dad. Their drinking shaped so much of how I viewed men in terms of love, and safety. I never knew which version of either man I would get — the one laughing and telling stories, or the one raging with slurred words and heavy hands. I saw how alcohol could turn someone you love into someone you feared. I learned that men were unpredictable, unsafe, and unstable. I had to walk on eggshells to cope. These experiences planted seeds of anxiety, distrust, and hypervigilance in me, robbing me of the innocence that every little girl deserves to have.

The Lord God Almighty has redefined and realigned what home looks like for me and my family. I have learned and experienced home as a state of being, not just a physical place. God has blessed my family and me to be "at home" in a house, an apartment, even a hotel where we stayed temporarily while our house was being built. My husband has always complimented me by telling me that no matter where we are, I make every place a home. The love, care, compassion, and intentionality flow freely from me because I know what lacking a place to call home did to me as a child.

Home is with my husband and my children. Home is seeing them as the treasures and blessings from God that they truly are. And in our home, there is fullness of joy.

REFLECTION QUESTIONS

1. What did "home" mean to you as a child?
2. Which places felt the most unsafe, and why?
3. Where did you feel the most loved and accepted?
4. How did moving between houses shape your need for stability and belonging as an adult?
5. What has God taught you regarding what true home means today?

PRAYER

Father God, thank You for being my eternal dwelling place when no house felt like home. Heal the scars of instability, loneliness, and fear from my childhood. Anchor my heart in You and teach me to build a home filled with Your presence, love, and peace. In Jesus' name, Amen.

DECLARATION

I am not homeless in my soul. God is my dwelling place. I am safe, secure, and deeply loved in Him.

The houses I lived in may have offered shelter, but they never gave me the safety of home. Each place left me feeling more like a visitor than a daughter, leaving me searching for something to anchor me

and remind me I belonged somewhere. But in the midst of all that abandonment, God began writing a story of hope, a journey that would take me from feeling abandoned to finally discovering what it means to be anchored.

MY SILENT REFLECTIONS

CHAPTER 6

From Abandoned to Anchored

Scripture Focus: Deuteronomy 31:6 (NIV)

Be strong and courageous. Do not be afraid or terrified because of them, for the Lord your God goes with you; he will never leave you nor forsake you.

Even when I was anchored in pain, abuse, and abandonment, God was already writing a story of belonging and redemption over my life.

For so long, my life felt anchored — but not anchored in safety, love, or security. I was anchored in trauma, abuse, neglect, and abandonment. The very places that were supposed to nurture and protect me became the breeding grounds for wounds that cut deep into my identity and my understanding of love.

Over time, I started believing the lie that a man would solve all my problems. I looked at men as potential tickets out, sources of value, rescuers. I was desperate for love and protection in any form, even if it was broken. My view of God was just as distorted. I saw Him as a distant figure, someone who owed me because of everything I had endured. I approached Him like He was Santa Claus instead of the Savior of the world, expecting Him to fix my pain without realizing He was calling me to relationship, not transactions.

But even in my brokenness, God never turned His back on me. He began to reveal Himself in ways I had never experienced. For the first time in my life, I began to feel acceptance that didn't come with strings attached. He surrounded me with other young ministers and a great college friend who was living boldly for Him. He placed an amazing village around me that supported me as I went to school and worked. We never lacked anything because His provision was constant and sure.

When I gave God my eternal yes and asked Him to come and live in my heart, everything truly shifted for me. For the first time in my life, I started to understand what it meant to be loved by a father in a relationship that wasn't rooted in performance, fear or abandonment. I felt affirmed by Him in ways I had never experienced from my earthly parents. He spoke to my soul and called me Daughter, Beloved, Chosen, and Redeemed. His love wrapped itself around my broken places and whispered to the little girl inside of me that she was safe, that she belonged, and that she would never be alone again. In His presence, I found an unshakeable identity and a deep assurance that I was fully seen, fully known, and fully loved.

As broken as I was, He held me close. I began to look forward to my future in a way I never had before. I found community. I found belonging. I found purpose. Even though I still lacked wisdom and understanding, His love sustained me. I learned His voice very early on after I gave Him my yes. It was during that season that I became rooted in a great church family — the kind of church in which the mothers would pull your coat tail, speak life into you, love you fiercely, and pray you under the benches all in the same breath.

The love of God began to wash away the deep stains of my trauma, layer by layer, like gentle waves cleansing the shore. For so long I had walked under the weight of shame and pain, but His love lifted that burden and set my feet on solid ground. My heart, once heavy with sorrow, now turned its gaze toward the things of heaven. He gave me a new song to sing ... a song of hope, redemption, and purpose. My outlook on life began to change in ways I never saw coming. Where there was despair, He planted joy. Where there was fear, He planted faith. And for the first time, I could see a future that wasn't defined by what happened to me but by who He is in me.

As I became anchored in Him, I began to understand what it truly meant to be a daughter of God. I learned that I could be loved by a Father who would never abandon me, who wasn't waiting for me to perform to earn His affection. This was a Father who knew me so intimately that He numbered every hair on my head (Luke 12:7). In His eyes, I was enough — even in my brokenness. I was precious, chosen, and worth dying for. To finally rest in a love that was unconditional and unwavering healed places in me I didn't even know were bleeding. I found safety in His embrace and discovered that being His daughter was the greatest identity I could ever carry.

I still had a lot of growing to do, but I was no longer abandoned. I was anchored in Him. All the while, God had His hand on me, loving me patiently, calling me deeper, and promising me that even if everyone else forsook me, He never would. He became the Anchor that steadied my soul when everything else failed.

REFLECTION QUESTIONS:

1. In what ways did abandonment shape how you saw God and others?
2. When did you first experience the unwavering love of God despite your brokenness?
3. How has God shown Himself as your Anchor in seasons of instability?
4. What lies did you believe about men or relationships because of your childhood experiences?
5. Where in your life do you need to replace broken anchors with Christ as your true Anchor today?

PRAYER

Heavenly Father,

Thank You for never abandoning me, even when I felt unloved and unseen. Thank You for being my Anchor when everything around me was shaking. Lord, heal every place in me that is still tethered to pain, abuse, and neglect. Help me release the lies I've believed about myself, men, and even You. Anchor me in Your truth, Your love, and Your unchanging Word. Let me stand firm in the security of knowing I am Yours. Today, I choose to cling to You above all else, trusting that You will never leave me nor forsake me. In Jesus' name, Amen.

DECLARATION

I declare that I am no longer anchored in pain, abandonment, or trauma. God is my Rock and my Anchor. His love sustains me, His truth sets me free, and His presence secures me in every season. I am not abandoned. I am held. I am loved. I am His.

Though I had found an anchor in God's love, the echoes of emptiness still reverberated through the chambers of my heart. I carried silent voids that words couldn't fill, and people couldn't soothe. As I stepped out of abandonment into His embrace, I realized that healing would require confronting the haunting echoes of emptiness that followed me into every relationship, every opportunity, and every dream.

MY SILENT REFLECTIONS

CHAPTER 7

Echoes of Emptiness

Scripture Focus: Isaiah 41:10 (NIV)

So do not fear, for I am with you; do not be dismayed, for I am your God. I will strengthen you and help you; I will uphold you with my righteous right hand.

It was about confronting the silent void within — the unspoken pain and unmet needs that echoed throughout my life — and about how God filled those hollow places with His love.

Emptiness has always had a sound in my life — like a heavy stone sinking to the bottom of my soul, pulling down every hope, dream, and desire I carried. It's been a dull ache that I could never find relief from. This emptiness had me in a chokehold at various moments throughout my life. There were times I could feel the tingling of emptiness running down my arms or feel it taking my breath away completely. It always showed up in the quiet moments when I wasn't distracted — when I had to sit with myself and face my pain.

Emptiness was there when my strength wasn't enough for a breakthrough. It showed up when I was frustrated that things weren't moving the way I wanted. It would spill over onto those I loved, causing confusion and chaos. I felt it for so long that I can't even pinpoint exactly when it first began. Maybe it was watching my mom move as a woman without stability or safety. Maybe it was being bounced between four different families, never knowing where I truly belonged. Maybe it started when I lost my mother as I knew her at age seven after her mental breakdown.

My emptiness was rooted in feeling unsafe, unheard, unseen, invalidated, and unaccepted. I was a daddy-less daughter who felt rejected by her own father. As I entered my formative years, emptiness only grew because no one poured into me. I was on my own, trying to figure out life in a confusing world. Seeing my friends enjoy simple everyday things that were out of my reach triggered loneliness, frustration, and a deep void.

I remember living in that small apartment with my mother, her boyfriend, and my siblings. It never felt like home — just four walls filled with tension, chaos, and my mother's reckless disregard for anyone's needs but her own. I felt that I didn't belong there, yet I carried the weight of trying to protect my siblings from her emotional storms. Night after night I cried myself to sleep, feeling silent screams rise from deep within me — screams no one ever heard. No help came. No one arrived to rescue me. The emptiness that lived inside me began to dictate every part of my life. I made choices I regret, including giving my body away in search of a connection. Promiscuity felt better than being invisible and alone.

I wanted validation so badly. But the ache continued; nothing seemed to lessen it.

In college, I chose to pledge a sorority because I longed for big sisters and a sense of belonging. I felt responsible for my younger siblings and therefore felt I had abandoned them by leaving home. I'd carried the burden of trying to protect them from what I wasn't protected from. So, the thought of having a sisterhood to look out for *me* was everything. But while it created a sense of belonging and gave me short-term validation to boost my self-esteem, my sorority did nothing to heal the holes in my heart.

The echoes of emptiness eventually impacted how I parented my children. As determined as I was not to be like my mom, I found myself doing some of the same things, parenting from a disconnected place. I was emotionally unavailable at times when they needed me. I took my frustrations out on them. For all my efforts, I just didn't know how to show up as a whole person. But I kept trying. Brokenness left me pouring from an empty cup, struggling to give what I didn't have. I had no idea how dangerous that really was. I didn't know that you cannot nourish others when your own well is dry. Eventually you will burn out, become resentful, or crumble under the weight of your own unmet needs.

I hid my emptiness well. It was insulated under the image I so carefully tended — gorgeous hair, beautiful clothes, charming personality, and ability to show up strong for others. But the emptiness led to strongholds, lies, and self-deception. I became a people-pleaser to distract myself from my dysfunction. I operated from a baseline of striving, performance, and desperation, rather than love, wisdom, and discernment. Being everything to everyone was my mantra. I poured and poured. I ran, walked, crawled, did whatever it took to not feel. But the emptiness never went away. When it surfaced to the point that I couldn't ignore it, I ran from people, places, and things that made me uncomfortable.

I had given my life to the Lord many years ago but was made to realize I had never fully let Him have my heart. I had a form of godliness but denied its power to change me. I held Him responsible for what my parents did to me. I held Him responsible for every hurt, even the self-inflicted pain. I didn't know how to fully receive love from my Heavenly Father because my earthly father had been such a poor example. My father threw me away. My mother threw me away. I didn't love me; therefore, I threw me away **too.** So, why would God want such a broken little girl? Why would He bother to care?

For years, I rode the highs of breakthrough moments, glimpsing God at work in my life. I knew He had called me, and I could see the gifts He had placed within me. Yet, true acceptance — real, unshakable intimacy with Him as my Father — always felt just out of reach. Beneath every prayer, every act of faith, there lurked a shadow I could never fully escape: the scars of trauma, the sharp sting of rejection, the hollow ache of abandonment, and the dark imprint of abuse. I learned to perform, to mold myself into the version I believed God and others wanted. But all the while, my breaking point simmered quietly beneath the surface — an invisible pressure building, threatening to shatter the carefully constructed life I showed the world.

In my early twenties, I was terrified that I would end up like my mother. I would cry in Tennyson's arms, haunted by the fear of mental illness and the generational curses I believed were waiting to claim me. I remember two breaking points vividly.

The first came when Tennyson and I broke up after our daughter was six months old. That moment shattered me. It was one of the lowest points in my life. All my dreams washed away in an instant, and I wanted to give up. I was tired of fighting — fighting to be seen, to be loved, to be enough. I had been in survival mode my entire life, and I didn't have anything left to go to war with. It felt like the rug had been snatched from under me once again, and I didn't have the tools to cope with the pain.

The second breaking point came years later, after Tennyson and I had married. We had already endured multiple miscarriages the year before … and then came the year we gave birth to a stillborn son. I don't know that words can ever fully describe what it feels like to give birth to a child who never takes a breath. When my obstetrician told us our son had passed away in the womb, something inside me fractured. I wanted to leap off that table and run, to escape the unbearable weight of reality.

In the days that followed, the darkness was relentless. I felt the pull of that generational curse whispering to me, tempting me to surrender — to give in, to make the pain stop. The enemy's voice sounded almost merciful: "It's okay to give in; the pain will end." And truthfully, escape felt easier than facing another day. I was tired. Hurting. Numb. Hollow. Even the love of my husband and children couldn't reach the deep places of my grief.

But mercy stepped in and said no. God spoke clearly to my heart: "Daughter, this is not your portion. Your latter will be greater. Don't give up, and don't give in." And somehow, through tears and trembling faith, I didn't.

The echoes of my emptiness played throughout my adulthood. I kept telling myself that it would be better when I got a better job, when I made more money, when I lost weight, when my kids got older, when we moved to a bigger home or got better cars. But I carried that broken girl — that broken, empty little girl from deep within — into each new place and each new season. She was the common denominator that made ***me*** the problem.

I had to accept the hard truth that I had spent my life fixing my own problems and being my own solutions. I was my own god. Now, let that sink in! I didn't give the Lord a chance to do much of anything for me. In ME did I put my faith, hope, and trust! Why? Because that's what my brokenness and trauma taught me to do. But dear God, how freeing it has been to finally reach a space where I don't have to have all the answers; where I can simply say, "I know my Father loves me and He is my very present help." I finally mean it, and it feels amazing!

I want my daughters and every woman I mentor to know that trauma healing is life work. Time does not heal all wounds; only our Heavenly father can do that! Every day, you must choose freedom and keep moving forward. There is healing, joy, and life beyond pain. Healing is a *journey* that will ebb and flow, not a *destination*. On the other side of your brokenness are better days ahead. It's okay to not be okay, but it's not okay to stay there.

This message is for every woman whose childhood wounds still whisper in her heart. I see you. I feel you. I want you to give yourself permission to stop running, stop hiding, and face every emotion, every ache, every lie, every mistake from your past — and rise stronger from it. There is a God who loves you with a relentless, unshakable love, who is waiting for you with open arms, ready to fill every empty place in your soul. You are worth turning to Him in full vulnerability. You are worth this journey. You are worth every tear, every step, every moment of courage. God wants you healed. God wants you whole. God wants you free, and nothing — not your past, not your pain, not the lies you've carried — can stop it.

I sit with women I counsel as a wounded healer, not as someone who has arrived or lived a perfect life. Not as someone who's got it all together, either. I've been beaten down, bruised, and almost destroyed by circumstances, but I am here today because of God's grace alone. He turned my pain into purpose, my heartache into hope, and my despair into destiny. I have done my work, and every day I have to make the choice to keep moving forward. And now He has allowed me to be a voice for broken little girls who became unhealed women.

REFLECTION QUESTIONS

1. Where does emptiness still try to show up in your life today?
2. How did emptiness shape the way you parented or built relationships?
3. What did you use to try to fill the void that only God could fill?
4. What does wholeness look like for you today?

PRAYER

Father, I bring every echo of emptiness within me to You. Thank You for being close to the brokenhearted and saving those crushed in spirit. Fill every void with Your love. Heal the wounds I've tried to ignore or cover. Help me walk in wholeness daily and pour out from a place of overflow. Silence the echoes of my pain and replace them with songs of Your hope and purpose. In Jesus' name, Amen.

DECLARATION

Today, I declare that I am no longer defined by the echoes of emptiness from my past. I am filled with the fullness of God. His love saturates every hollow place within me. I am whole, I am healed, and I am free. I walk forward in purpose, anchored in the truth that I am deeply loved, seen, and chosen by God. Amen.

The emptiness within me carried whispers of pain I couldn't quite name, but as I listened closer, I realized those whispers were rooted in lies ... lies that trauma had told me for as long as I could remember. Moving from the haunting echoes of emptiness, I began to uncover truth: My emptiness not only lay in the absence of love or safety; it was filled with the deception of trauma that shaped how I saw myself, my God, and my entire world.

MY SILENT REFLECTIONS

CHAPTER 8

Trauma Lied to Me

Scripture Focus: John 8:32 (NIV)

Then you will know the truth, and the truth will set you free.

Unhealed trauma shapes the world of a child in ways they can't even articulate. It colors their view of themselves, their worth, their safety, their future. Trauma teaches them distorted truths that become their reality — until those lies are confronted by God's truth and love.

From the time I was a little girl, trauma taught me fear and insecurity. Trauma taught me to normalize the dysfunction of not having a dad in my life. Trauma taught me to be afraid and keep secrets. Trauma taught me that I was not safe. Trauma taught me that living in the projects, having babies, and living on welfare was the life I should expect. Trauma taught me to trust in myself only. Trauma taught me that men hurt little girls. Trauma taught me that men beat their wives and girlfriends. Trauma made me think that my mom's mental health issues were my fault ("If only I'd been a better child ... ."). Trauma taught me to normalize mental health issues in my family and expect the same thing to happen to me.

"See to it that no one falls short of the grace of God and that no bitter root grows up to cause trouble and defile many." — Hebrews 12:15 (NIV)

Trauma is like a cruel teacher, shaping how we think and feel. Research shows that 61% of adults report experiencing at least one Adverse Childhood Experience (ACE), and nearly 1 in 6 have had four or more (CDC, 2021). These traumatic events — neglect, abuse, family dysfunction — increase the risk of depression, anxiety, substance abuse, and chronic disease later in life (CDC, 2023).

"Above all else, guard your heart, for everything you do flows from it." — Proverbs 4:23

Trauma and my upbringing taught me that mothers and daughters don't have good relationships, which is why I wanted to be a "boy mom" so badly: I was afraid of the destruction that could come from trying to raise a daughter. Trauma taught me that my life would be better if I were someone else. Trauma taught me low self-worth and low self-esteem. Trauma taught me to accept any and everything from a man just so I could have someone to call my own.

When trauma is left unhealed, it becomes the lens through which we interpret life — distorting our view of love, safety, relationships, and even our identity.

"For now we see only a reflection as in a mirror; then we shall see face to face." — 1 Corinthians 13:12a (NIV)

Trauma told me I wasn't good enough. Trauma told me I was responsible for all the bad things that happened to my brothers and sisters because I left home for college. Trauma taught me family dysfunction, molestation, abuse. Trauma taught me to swing first and ask questions later. Trauma taught me emotional instability. Trauma taught me to settle, to not have standards, to carry shame and guilt. Trauma told me that the only way to stop all the madness was to end my life. And when my suicide attempt failed at age 15, trauma tormented me for years with the threat of dying young. Trauma taught me to protect myself, to lie and manipulate for survival. It taught me to run at 100 miles an hour to avoid feeling pain.

Studies reveal that exposure to multiple ACEs increases the likelihood of mental health issues by up to fourfold (Felitti et al., 1998). I lived that reality — my thoughts were constantly clouded by trauma's lies, and I was convinced that my life was hopelessly broken.

One of the deepest lies trauma whispered to me was that food could comfort what was broken inside. Food became my safe place, my reward, my numbing tool, and my silent friend. It was there when people weren't. It didn't judge me, hurt me, or leave me — at least that's what I thought. But while food was a great comforter, it turned out to be a terrible friend. Food told me it could soothe my sadness. That extra cookie or slice of cake told me it could quiet my anxiety. Late-night runs to the pantry told me that food could fill the void left by rejection and loneliness. But every time the last bite was gone, the guilt, shame, and self-loathing remained — and often grew louder. Trauma lied to me, convincing me that eating could heal my pain when it only buried it deeper beneath more layers of bondage.

Statistics

- Over 40% of adults with binge eating disorder report that their eating behaviors are directly linked to past trauma or PTSD (Udo & Grilo, 2018).
- Approximately 70% of women with emotional eating struggles say they began using food to cope in childhood or adolescence, often as a result of abuse, neglect, or household dysfunction (Van Strien & Ouwens, 2007).
- Emotional eating is strongly correlated with childhood emotional neglect and maternal rejection, both of which leave lasting imprints on self-worth and coping skills (NEDA, 2022).

“For he satisfies the longing soul, and the hungry soul he fills with good things.” — Psalm 107:9 (ESV)

True satisfaction can only come from the One who created your soul. Food was never meant to be my healer — God is. Food was never meant to be my comforter — the Holy Spirit is. Food was never meant to be my source — Jehovah Jireh is.

At times, the echoes of emptiness were so loud I felt like I was suffocating. Trauma told me I would end up just like my mom and lose my mind. Trauma told me that a man would never stay; that I wasn't enough for my husband, and he would eventually walk out like everyone else. It distorted my view of God, whispering that He wasn't really good and that He didn't care about me.

“He heals the brokenhearted and binds up their wounds.” — Psalm 147:3 (NIV)

Trauma told me that playing house and cohabiting with my child's father was the closest I was going to get to the family I wanted. Trauma taught me anger, vindictiveness, the urge to fight to keep from letting anyone step on me again or make me feel small. Trauma taught me that having a piece of a man was better than having no man at all. Trauma taught me desperation and manipulation.

Trauma that is not transformed will always be transferred — to relationships, marriages, parenting, and every place we try to show up as whole while silently bleeding.

“He punishes the children and their children for the sin of the parents to the third and fourth generation.” — Exodus 34:7b (NIV)

Trauma's impact is pervasive. The National Child Traumatic Stress Network highlights the fact that trauma affects brain development, emotional regulation, and relational capacity (National Child Traumatic Stress Network, n.d.). It creates strongholds in the mind — patterns of thinking and believing that keep us trapped in cycles of fear, rejection, anger, and shame. A wounded child who never finds healing grows into an adult who builds walls instead of bridges, carries fear instead of faith, and often repeats the cycles they desperately wanted to escape.

Even after I gave my life to the Lord, trauma lied and told me my healing would come through finding a husband. Trauma told me to expect to be hurt, and to hurt others back with interest. But God came in and redeemed my life from every lie and every seed of destruction. Where the enemy sowed deception and built strongholds, God came in and showed me the truth of who I was in Him. What Satan meant for evil, God turned around for good.

Pain that is never processed becomes the silent dictator of our choices, convincing us that survival is the best we can hope for, when God has called us to thrive.

"The thief comes only to steal and kill and destroy; I have come that they may have life, and have it to the full." — John 10:10 (NIV)

Trauma lied to me and told me I had to be in control to survive. Having had parents who failed me and left me vulnerable, I learned to tightly grip anything I felt I could manage on my own. Control became my shield, my way of regulating emotions I could not understand. Thus, it created a false sense of safety from the storms around me. I built walls and burned bridges—whatever it took to keep me safe.

Fear is torment and it had me bound. When I couldn't be in control, I felt like I was unraveling — and at times, I truly did lose control. What I didn't realize is that this was a stronghold rooted in abandonment, abuse, and neglect. But to God be the glory — He opened my eyes to see that control was not protection, it was bondage. Real freedom is found surrendering to Him. The Word says, "For God has not given us the spirit of fear, but of power and of love and a sound mind" (2 Timothy 1:7, NKJV).

When I finally released control into His hands, I began to discover the safety, love, and peace I had been searching for all along. But, even with that freedom, I realized yet another battled that lingered — a battle with my own self-image. I spent so many years wishing, hoping, praying, doubting, and wavering. I didn't want to be disappointed, and I didn't want to disappoint God. I believed that I had failed God as His daughter. I felt unworthy, convinced that redemption was beyond my reach. I believed my mistakes, my pain, and my flaws made me unacceptable, that I could never measure up and be deserving of the love of a Holy God! But now I know better. I thank Him that every lie has been canceled; every stronghold torn down. The lies have been replaced with truth. The enemy has been exposed as the fraud, liar, cheater, and disruptor he has been in my life since I was a little girl.

For so many years, the lies were like elevator music in the background of my life — always playing, always humming, shaping every decision and emotion. I knew they weren't true, but I didn't know how to shut them off. My breaking point came when God showed me that the little girl inside me was still hurting, still stuck in her trauma. That revelation changed everything and put me on a path to rescue her.

I didn't have to keep believing the lies. And neither do you.

I had to be intentional about replacing those lies with His truth. It's a daily choice. A discipline. A battle. But the truth really does set us free. I've learned that I am enough because He is enough. I've learned that His love is not based on my performance, my past, or my pain. It is rooted in who He is — my Father, my Redeemer, my Healer.

Through God's Word, prayer, counseling, and the resulting inner healing, I began tearing down the strongholds trauma had built in my mind and in my spirit. The Substance Abuse and Mental Health

Services Administration, or SAMHSA, emphasizes that trauma-informed care includes realizing the impact of trauma, recognizing signs and symptoms, and responding with supportive healing environments (SAMHSA, 2014a).

Trauma told me so many lies, but God's truth has set me free.

I'm not completely where I want to be, but I am no longer where I used to be. My journey is not complete, but I am well on my way to total freedom.

- Psalm 139:14 (NIV) — I praise you because I am fearfully and wonderfully made; your works are wonderful; I know that full well.
- Jeremiah 1:5a (NIV) — Before I formed you in the womb I knew you, before you were born I set you apart.
- Numbers 23:19 (NIV) — God is not human, that he should lie, not a human being, that he should change his mind. Does he speak and then not act? Does he promise and not fulfill?

REFLECTION QUESTIONS

1. What lies has trauma taught you about yourself, your worth, or your future?
2. How have these lies impacted your choices, relationships, and self-perception?
3. What truths from God's Word directly confront these lies?
4. In what areas of your life are you still allowing trauma's **lies** to be louder than God's voice?
5. What would your life look like if you fully believed God's truth over every lie?
6. In what areas of your life are you still holding on to control out of fear, and how do you surrender those places to God to experience His peace?

PRAYER

Heavenly Father, Thank You for revealing the lies trauma has taught me. I repent for believing words and thoughts that do not align with Your truth. Heal the broken little girl inside of me. Tear down every stronghold that keeps me bound. Replace every lie with Your Word and renew my mind daily. I choose to trust You as my Father, my Healer, and my Redeemer. Help me to walk in freedom and teach others the same. In Jesus' name, Amen.

DECLARATION

I declare that I am no longer bound by the lies of trauma. God's truth has set me free. I am loved, accepted, and seen by Him. Every stronghold is broken in the name of Jesus, and I walk boldly into my future, healed, whole, and anchored in the unshakable truth of my Father's love.

Trauma may have lied to me for years, but God's love told me the truth. As I began to tear down the strongholds that kept me bound, He started showing me glimpses of His redemptive plan — not just for my life, but for my heart, my marriage, and my family.

In the middle of my brokenness, God sent me a love story I never imagined I could have. A love that would reflect His faithfulness and teach me what it really means to be seen, chosen, and cherished.

As you turn the page, come with me into Chapter 9, where I share how God's redemptive love met me in the most unexpected way — and how He used 25 years of marriage to rewrite the narrative trauma tried to leave behind.

MY SILENT REFLECTIONS

CHAPTER 9

God's Redemptive Love

Scripture Focus: 1 Peter 5:10 (NIV)

And the God of all grace, who called you to his eternal glory in Christ, after you have suffered a little while, will himself restore you and make you strong, firm and steadfast.

When God's redemptive love steps in, He takes the shattered pieces of your past and builds a masterpiece that reflects His glory.

I was always determined and stubborn because I had to be. As a child with no control, my pursuit of love and having someone to call my own knew no bounds. Denied so much in life, I decided romantic love and companionship would not be among those denials.

Marriage was always on my radar. Even as a little girl, the thought of having my own family one day kept me going when life felt unbearable. Growing up, I dreamed of my beautiful wedding and what it would be like to be a wife — to have someone to call my own. But my reality never matched my dreams. My mother and stepfather didn't model healthy marriage; neither did my dad and his wife. I saw a few healthy marriages in the distance, but not on a daily basis. Still, the desire to have my own family remained deep in my soul.

I started dating very young. I was only 12 and in 7th grade when I went to my first school dance with my then-boyfriend, Vernell. I had no business dating or even *looking* at boys, but by 8th grade I'd even dated a drug dealer. He was very well known, and a lot of girls liked him, but he set his sights on me. The attention excited me, but fear lingered. Throughout junior high and high school, I chased the wrong types: the pretty boys, the roughnecks, the unavailable, and the abusive. I allowed myself to be used, abused, and pierced through with many sorrows as I searched for the love of my father in teenage boys.

Meeting my future husband, Tennyson, at a young age showed me both God's sovereignty and His sense of humor. We had crossed paths for years — I passed him on the school bus during two years of high school without ever saying a word to him. It wasn't until college that a genuine friendship began to form, built on trust and mutual admiration. Tennyson became a true confidant and safe space for me. He was the first genuine guy who showed up for me without expecting anything in return.

One day, while we were spending time with one of his friends, our friendship took an unexpected turn: We realized we were attracted to each other. That night, as we danced, something in me shifted. The way he held me made me feel a connection I had never experienced before. I felt protected.

What followed was a whirlwind courtship. Tennyson was unlike anyone I had ever dated — kind, compassionate, chivalrous, and well-liked by everyone. Although he was in a fraternity, he was not the typical frat guy; I had already been there and done that. Instead, he treated me with respect, always putting me first. So, I dove headfirst into a relationship with him, ready for a love that would last.

Tennyson and I dated for only a few short months, but he was everything I had ever wanted in a guy — qualities I had searched for but never found. As our first Christmas together approached, he decided to stay in our college town to work, while I headed back home to spend time with my younger siblings. I had been feeling a little off in my body —some dizzy spells here and there — but I brushed it off. *No, it can't be that. I'm not pregnant,* I told myself.

On Christmas Day, at my mom's house surrounded by my siblings, I decided to take a test. I was about two weeks late, but I chalked it up to the stress of finals. Still, something in me knew I needed to be sure. I slipped into the bathroom and waited for what felt like hours, to see if a plus or minus would appear. Sure enough — it was positive! A rush of excitement filled me, quickly followed by fear. I was thrilled at the thought of becoming a mother and having a family of my own. I wanted a little boy. I told myself I would be a better boy mom than a girl mom. I had not seen many healthy mother-daughter relationships growing up, and I didn't want to repeat what I had witnessed.

Despite my fears, my pregnancy was one of the most beautiful seasons of my life. I had minimal morning sickness and felt radiant in my body. My hair grew longer than ever, and my nails were the strongest they had ever been. I joyfully walked the college campus, "bouncing around" and glowing, all the way into my ninth month. Through it all, Tennyson was right there ... loving, supportive, and just as excited as I was.

And as much as I feared having a little girl, that is exactly the abundant blessing God gave me. What I didn't realize at the time was that I needed my beautiful Imari just as much as she needed me. From the moment she arrived, I poured myself feverishly — and fearfully — into being a good mom. I did what I thought a good mom should do. I was trying to live out a love that had never been shown to me, reaching for grace I had never experienced firsthand, but that God was slowly teaching me to embody.

But almost immediately, my emotional wounds began to surface. I didn't know how to balance a relationship, care for my daughter, and wrestle with the unhealed and unacknowledged trauma within me. I could not call my mom to ask for advice or receive love or any type of encouragement. I had to figure this thing out for myself … and I was failing miserably.

I wanted this family so badly. I wanted Tennyson. But honestly, I wanted him to make up for every man who had hurt me, including my father. The truth was that I was deeply in need of healing — and I didn't even know it.

Tennyson and I broke up when our daughter was six months old. I felt alone, shattered, and terrified of failing her. Playing house without commitment left me broken, and when he moved out of the home we shared, I felt abandoned all over again. I worked menial jobs and lived paycheck to paycheck, depressed and hopeless. Tennyson was a good dad, but co-parenting with him was torture for my broken heart.

Out of fear, pain, and vindictiveness, I took Imari and ran to another city. I didn't let Tennyson see her for three months. He was prepared, as I thought he would be, to take me to court for his rights to his daughter, so I had to put my issues and my pride aside and allow my child time with her father. But, as he and I reconnected for visits, I continued to spiral.

In my darkest place, I cried out to God. I went to church one morning knowing that if I didn't give my life to Christ that day, I wouldn't make it. I had been feeling this unrest in my spirit and could not understand what it meant. At the altar I gave my life to Christ not just for myself, but for my baby girl. Imari deserved a mommy who was healed, well, and whole. I had to pick up the pieces and demonstrate something for my daughter that I had never experienced. The only way that was going to be possible was with the help of my Heavenly Father.

As my faith grew and God became the center of my life, I committed to abstinence and to waiting on His best for me. Co-parenting with

Tennyson improved, and we became great friends again. He even moved to my city to help with Imari.

It wasn't long before our feelings for each other reignited. Full transparency: At that time, I was distracted by another guy who was telling me everything I wanted to hear. So, I gave Tennyson a really hard time. When he began hinting at us getting back together, then talking of marriage, I told him no at first, wanting him to hurt like I had been hurt. I was on my high horse, guarded and confused ... not realizing that sometimes we can want something for so long, then when it finally comes, we can't accept that it's real.

A few months prior, I had made a vow to the Lord. I wanted to be married, but I did not want my daughter to have a stepfather. I would never put my child through that miserable existence. I told God I would not dishonor Him by giving Him a laundry list of what I was looking for in a man. I told Him, "You made me; you know what's best for me. Send me your best!" Imagine my shock when God's best for me turned out to be the man with whom I already had a child!

Just as I was about to give up hope on our family ever being together, Tennyson proposed. It was surreal, a whirlwind of emotions, but my heart was his as it always had been. I never stopped loving him. But I still wasn't sure. I didn't know whether I could take the disappointment if I once again lost the family I wanted so much. I asked him for some time and space to figure this out.

Tennyson left town for the weekend, and we had no contact. We met up when he returned. I sat in my car with him and gave him a long speech about how I'd always love him, but that we should focus on co-parenting and just being friends. My rehearsed speech went on and on. Seeing the disappointment in his face as he got out of the car stunned me. As he drove away that night in the Kroger parking lot and his taillights disappeared into the darkness, something shifted inside of me. What had I just done? I thought, *Girl, you love this man! You do want your family with him!*

I drove back to my apartment in silence, my heart heavy, my mind racing. That night I tossed and turned, unable to escape the war inside me. By morning, I picked up the phone and called Tennyson. He didn't hesitate — he came straight over. We began to talk. Looking me in the eyes, he asked, "Would you be willing to go to marriage counseling with me?" I didn't know if I was ready, but something in me said yes.

After just one session, everything changed. The walls between us shattered. We spoke with raw honesty as we discussed what we wanted, the ways we had both failed, how desperately we longed for restoration. The pastor looked at me and said, "The anger you're carrying toward him isn't really about him." His words cut deep. He was right. My rage wasn't against Tennyson — it was the echo of wounds that had never healed.

Then Tennyson turned to me, his voice trembling, and confessed, "From the very first time I called your apartment back in college, I knew you were my wife." Hearing that both broke me *and* **yet** pieced me back together. The pastor told Tennyson that it was time to stop running.

That night, our journey back to each other truly began. On the drive to pick up our daughter, we poured out every secret, every failure, every truth. The next day, I closed the door on the other guy for good. Six weeks later, Tennyson and I stood at the altar before God, vowing to build the life we nearly lost as husband and wife. Just a month later, cheered on by my husband and our bright-eyed, three-year-old daughter, I walked across the stage to receive my bachelor's degree in respiratory therapy.

We'd had a lot of bumps in the road after having our daughter and breaking up. We'd definitely put the cart before the horse. But God gave us a loving marriage.

As beautiful as our life together has been, the early years of marriage were a struggle for me through no fault of Tennyson's. I was a broken little girl who was now a wife and mom. I thought the demons of my past would go away. No ... they were right there with me.

But you know who else was with me? My husband. He delivered on every promise. He didn't leave when I was being a handful. He took the hits and the darts I threw and wouldn't let me push him away. He never took it personally. He loved me through it all.

Defying the Odds

Our story defies statistics. In the United States, only 38% of African American children live in two-parent households, compared to 77% of non-Hispanic White children (U.S. Census Bureau, 2020). The divorce rate for African American couples remains high, and almost 50% of all U.S. marriages end in divorce (American Psychological Association, 2019). Yet, despite what the numbers say, here we are almost 25 years later, still choosing each other daily. Research shows that stable, loving relationships can help heal trauma (Johnson, 2004). Having a partner who is emotionally safe and supportive reduces the severity of PTSD symptoms, depression, and anxiety (Reddy et al., 2014). Marriage built on faith and commitment becomes a sacred covering, redeeming the pain of the past.

I have been showered by God's love through my husband. This man loves me from the heart of Jesus. The Bible tells us, "A cheerful heart is good medicine" (Proverbs 17:22a, NIV). Throughout our journey together, we've always received our daily dose of joy, which has strengthened our beautiful friendship and created a healthy, life-giving environment in our home. We've raised two amazing children, one still at home. Each is so unique. Our adopted daughter looks so much like us that you would never know she is adopted unless we told you. We've always been a tight-knit, hands-on, fun-loving family. Not a perfect family by any means, but a family standing together, no matter what.

The hardest seasons of our marriage came with the loss of our son through stillborn birth, as well as with job losses. Tennyson loved me through cancer and kept everything going while I recovered. We lived paycheck to paycheck in the early years, with as little as $25 in our account, but God always provided. My husband is the most grounded, faithful, loving, and loyal man I have ever met. We have been through the fire! But it has always been us as a team ... us against the world, so to speak. His unwavering faith carried me when my faith was frail. On many a night, Tennyson held me and wiped my tears away. He prayed for me when I was scared. I learned I could trust the God living inside of him.

God used my marriage to redeem His love inside of me. He used my husband's love to pull me out of darkness. I almost missed the blessing of a love that knows no bounds, looking at Ishmael instead of Isaac, the promise. Ishmael represents the counterfeit. He was not Abraham's promised heir. He came before the promised son, but he wasn't it. If you are not careful, you will fall for Ishmael. He may look right, sound right, even smell right, but be careful, he is not it. My husband is not only my Isaac; he is my Boaz. His banner over me has always been love.

As we approach 25 years of marriage, I look forward to spending more years with him — our taking more cruises together, watching our children walk in their full potential, welcoming our grandchildren, experiencing total freedom spiritually, mentally, physically, and financially. We've defied the odds. Some expected us to fail. But what God has joined together, no man can put asunder. God's love redeemed us!

REFLECTION QUESTIONS

1. In what areas of your life have you struggled to believe that God's love could redeem and restore what was broken?
2. How has your understanding of love and relationships been shaped by your past pain?
3. Where can you invite God's redemptive love to heal the deepest wounds of your heart today?
4. What does it mean to you personally that God never stops pursuing you, no matter how far you've wandered?
5. How has God shown you glimpses of His redemptive love through people, circumstances, or unexpected blessings?
6. What steps can you take to walk confidently in the truth that you are fully loved, fully forgiven, and fully redeemed?

PRAYER

Heavenly Father,

Thank You for Your redemptive love that never gives up on me. Thank You that even when I felt unworthy, unseen, or unlovable, You still called me Yours. Heal every place in my heart that has been shattered by rejection, abandonment, or betrayal. Restore my hope and teach me how to love from a place of wholeness. Help me to see myself through Your eyes — redeemed, chosen, and loved beyond measure. May Your love continue to rewrite my story for Your glory. In Jesus' mighty name, Amen.

DECLARATION

I declare that God's redemptive love has rewritten my story. I am loved, chosen, and cherished beyond measure. I declare that my marriage and family are blessed, covered, and anchored in Christ now and forever. Our love is rooted in His unshakable foundation, and no weapon formed against us shall prosper. We will thrive in unity, purpose, and **an** unbreakable covenant all the days of our lives.

As I reflect on God's redemptive love in my life and marriage, I am reminded that true healing goes beyond our relationships with others. The deepest work begins within. In the next chapter, I'll share how I learned that in order to heal my life, I had to go back and first allow God to heal the little girl inside me …

MY SILENT REFLECTIONS

CHAPTER 10

Heal Her to Heal Me

Scripture Focus: Jeremiah 17:14 (NIV)

Heal me, Lord, and I will be healed; save me and I will be saved, for you are the one I praise.

Matthew 18:3 (NIV)

And he said: Truly I tell you, unless you change and become like little children, you will never enter the kingdom of heaven.

My freedom required going back to rescue the little girl still suffocating under years of trauma, pain, and secrets. Healing her began to unlock the abundant life waiting for me today.

If you fly on an airplane often enough, you know the safety instructions by heart. As the flight attendant goes through the safety measures, she says with calm confidence, "In the event of a sudden drop in cabin pressure, oxygen masks will fall from the ceiling. Place the mask over your nose and mouth, secure it with the elastic band, and breathe normally. If you are traveling with a child or someone who requires assistance, secure your own mask first before helping others."

At first glance, that seems selfish. Why wouldn't I immediately help my child? Why would I not reach over to cover the face of someone I love before I put my own mask on? As I've gotten older, I realize the wisdom in this instruction. If you pass out from lack of oxygen, you are of no help to anyone. Your ability to save someone else's life depends entirely on your ability to help yourself first.

That instruction hit me deeply one day when I was in a counseling session with my personal therapist. God showed me that for so much of my life, I had been trying to save everyone else —rescue my siblings, heal my mother, fix the broken places in my family, parent my children better than I was parented, hold up my husband, be strong for everyone. But I was gasping for air myself.

God revealed that I could not keep running through life without putting the oxygen mask on my own soul. And He showed me that the little seven-year-old girl inside of me was suffocating. She had been without air for so long, trying to survive the trauma of losing her mother and being abandoned by her father. She needed healing, love, validation, safety, and hope. Adult me was still carrying her pain, in silence, unknowingly.

That's when I realized the oxygen mask wasn't just for me today. It was not just for my present struggles. We all have struggles. The oxygen mask was for her — for the little girl in me who was frozen in time, waiting for someone to rescue her, waiting for someone to tell her it was okay to breathe, to cry, to hope, to live. Until I went back and put the mask on that seven-year-old little girl, I would never be free to inhale the fullness of God's love, exhale all the pain I'd been holding in, and walk in the freedom He destined for me.

Healing is possible.
The little girl within us is worth rescuing.
Our broken places birth our greatest ministry.

LETTER TO MY YOUNGER SELF

Dear Little Miss Meka,

I intentionally call you "Little Miss" because you were never treated like a princess. You've been a whole bucket of sass since you came into the world. I write this letter to let you know that I am coming back for you. You are seven years old, and you've already seen so much. Thus far, you have not let it rob you, but eventually, it will.

I know you're scared and confused. You've seen domestic violence in multiple homes. You even saw a man beat a woman on the street in broad daylight. You just saw your mother have a mental breakdown right in front of you. That image will never leave your mind. You aren't even sure what has happened. You will not be able to reconcile the pain and trauma of the loss you suffered that day — losing your mom emotionally and mentally, even though she will still be alive for years to come. She will never be the same, and neither will you.

You will struggle to mature emotionally because of secrets you're too young to process. At this tender age, you're not even sure what to do with the shame, so you push it down. You won't realize for another 18 years that you've been molested. You will fear everything and not know how to trust anybody. You will become very guarded as a way to protect yourself. You will feel like a stranger in your own home.

In a few years, your dad will come home from prison. At first, spending time with him alone will terrify you. You don't understand a man's touch, voice, or affirming love for his daughter. All you know is that men hurt little girls because of what you and your cousins have experienced. But as your relationship with your dad grows, you'll find moments of relief, though they will be short-lived moments that will disappear when he gets married.

Your mother will keep moving you around the city throughout your formative years, making you insecure and teaching you not to get attached to people, places, or things. In grade school, you will lose your paternal grandmother — your anchor — and soon your dad's family will dissipate across the country, leaving you alone and without the support and love you need.

High school will be traumatizing. You will feel unseen, unworthy, disconnected. You'll lose your virginity at a young age to a boy you don't even like — because you crave acceptance and validation. As your dad builds his new family of boys, you will feel left out, like a mistake. You will keep trying to find love in the wrong places, believing that giving your body is the only way to receive love. Your mom will fail to show up when you need her most. She will miss your high school graduation, choosing her boyfriend over you. That will cut deep, but you'll bury it. You will keep going, keep performing, keep pushing ... and no one will see the girl dying inside.

College will seem to be your escape, but your pain will follow. Your pain will weigh you down for decades to come. You will make mistakes, face heartbreaks, become a struggling single mother. You will give your life to the Lord, but freedom will still feel out of reach. Strongholds will weigh you down, and the lies of trauma will scream louder than truth for years.

But today, Little Miss Meka, I have come to rescue you.

I am here to put the oxygen mask on you so that you can finally breathe. Take a slow deep breath in ... 4, 3, 2, 1 … now exhale slowly and completely. You are safe now, baby girl. I'm not leaving you behind. Just like the military vows to leave no man behind, I am here to rescue you. I am here to free you from emotional eating, perfectionism, anger, rejection, fear, and guilt. You've carried these burdens, and so many others, like a 50-pound sack of bricks on your soul for far too long. But today, with the help of our Almighty Father, I've come to help you lay it all down and break every chain of bondage. It's time to let it go and receive His peace and healing.

You will learn that you are His beautiful daughter, made on purpose for purpose. You will learn to laugh again. You will see yourself as God sees you. You will no longer be a slave to fear. You will realize that life is something that happens *for* you, not *to* you. You need a lifeline today. Please hear me: Life will not always be as it is right now. You are not stuck. You are seen and you are valuable. There is greatness inside of you waiting to bloom. You can rest safely in the love of your Heavenly Father, whose eyes have always been upon you with compassion and purpose.

One day, you will walk in the fullness of joy — healed and whole. You will learn to love and appreciate yourself from a pure place, free from shame and fear. You are enough. The things that happened to you were never your fault. God will turn every tragedy into triumph and use your story to become a beacon of hope for countless women.

You will one day become a faithful, loving wife. God will bless you with daughters and a son. Your firstborn daughter will be a light in your life, bringing healing to wounds you didn't even know were still open. She will anchor you in joy when the world around you feels like it's falling apart. As she grows into the beautiful woman God created her to be, the two of you will become friends, sharing a connection you never had with your own mother: a bond rooted in love, truth, and safety. You will treasure your adult relationships with your children more than anything else in this world. Your son will grow to be a mighty man of God. He will be your twin in every way as he will challenge you at times, but he will also fill your life with laughter, pride, and an unshakable love. And just when you think your heart can't hold anymore, God will entrust you with the honor of mothering a broken little girl through adoption. She will be one whose pain mirrors your own. You will help pull her from the grip of trauma and watch God restore her piece by piece, just as He did with you.

You will grow into a dynamic powerhouse, a woman of stature, a woman who commands every room she walks into. You will become a woman of whom people stand up and take notice — and not just because of your beauty, but because of the Spirit of the Lord that radiates from you. Your posture will be strong, and the confidence with which you carry yourself will be unshakeable. And when you reach that pinnacle of freedom, you will be unstoppable.

Sweet girl, you need to know this; you've had a real enemy from the very beginning. One who's tried to silence your voice and smother your purpose since your childhood. But today, everything changes. Today, you sound the alarm. Today, you rise. Your voice is no longer buried under shame or fear: It's a weapon, and it's free. You get to breathe deeply. You get to dance without apology. You get to laugh from your belly and rest in the arms of a Father who has always had a divine plan for your life. Fear no longer owns you. Trauma no longer defines you. Take a deep breath in, exhale, and let loose a victory shout! You are free, and your freedom is about to set others free as well!

The Spirit of the Sovereign Lord is upon me, because the Lord has anointed me to proclaim good news to the poor. He has sent me to bind up the brokenhearted, to proclaim freedom for the captives and release from darkness for the prisoners. — Isaiah 61:1 (NIV)

Never forget, precious one, your freedom is your inheritance. And as you journey to freedom and healing, know that you are never alone ... because when you get to the place where you have longed to be your entire life, I will be right here waiting to welcome you home.

With eternal love and open arms …

Your future self,
Adult Meka

REFLECTION QUESTIONS

1. Who is your "Little Miss" (or "Little Mister") that still needs healing and validation?
2. What traumas from childhood still impact your decisions, emotions, or relationships today?
3. When was the last time you felt joy like a child? What robbed you of that freedom?
4. In what ways have you tried to help others before helping yourself?
5. What does putting the oxygen mask on yourself look like in this season of your healing journey?

PRAYER

Father,

Thank You for revealing to me the little girl inside who still needs love, safety, and freedom. I ask You to meet her right where she is. Heal every wound, every memory, every trauma. Wrap Your loving arms around her and remind her that she is Yours. Help me to walk boldly in this healing journey so I can become the woman You created me to be. I choose to put my mask on first so I can love others from a place of wholeness. In Jesus' name, Amen.

DECLARATION

I declare that I am healed from the inside out. I will go back and rescue the little girl within me and give her the love, validation, and safety she deserved. I am no longer a prisoner of my past. I am whole, I am free, and I walk in the fullness of who God created me to be.

As I close this chapter of healing the little girl within me, I feel her inhale deeply for the first time in decades. She can finally breathe.

And because she can breathe, so can I. But healing isn't just about looking back — it's about moving forward. It's about choosing every day to walk in freedom, wholeness, and purpose.

You've journeyed with me through the silent cries, the echoes of emptiness, the lies trauma told, and the beauty of God's redemptive love. But there's still one chain left to break-- unforgiveness. The freedom you seek hinges on the ability to forgive. Let's walk into this next chapter together and unlock the power that will set you completely free.

MY SILENT REFLECTIONS

CHAPTER 11

Unchained – The Healing Power of Forgiveness

Scriptures Focus:

Ephesians 4:32 (NIV)

Be kind and compassionate to one another, forgiving each other, just as in Christ God forgave you.

Colossians 3:13 (NLT)

Make allowance for each other's faults and forgive anyone who offends you. Remember, the Lord forgave you, so you must forgive others.

Matthew 6:14-15 (NIV)

For if you forgive other people when they sin against you, your heavenly Father will also forgive you. But if you do not forgive others their sins, your Father will not forgive your sins.

Forgiveness is not about letting others off the hook; it is about setting yourself free from the chains of bitterness and pain.

Forgiveness. The word alone used to make my stomach turn. For so many years, it felt unfair to let go of the pain others caused me. I carried bitterness, anger, and resentment like a badge of honor — proof that what they did hurt me deeply. I thought holding on to unforgiveness was my way of making them pay. But the truth is, unforgiveness never punished them — it only kept me in chains.

They say unforgiveness is like drinking poison and waiting for the other person to die. That was my life. Each day I swallowed the toxic memories, thinking I was protecting myself, but all I was doing was slowly destroying my own peace. For years, I didn't realize that my inability to forgive my mother for her harsh words and abusive hands, or my father for his absence, or even myself for my mistakes, was eating away at my soul. Every time I thought I had moved on, a trigger would bring the anger and sadness right back to the surface. I was bound by invisible chains I didn't even realize were there.

But God … He specializes in the broken, messy places of our lives. He showed me that forgiveness isn't about excusing what happened or pretending it didn't hurt. Forgiveness is about setting yourself free from the grip of the past so you can embrace the future He has for you.

For so long, I believed unforgiveness was a shield to protect me from being hurt again, but it was really a shackle draining my strength and joy. When I finally released forgiveness over those who hurt me — and over myself — I felt those bonds shatter in the unseen realm. I felt lighter. I felt peace. I felt God's touch and His smile over me.

Forgiveness doesn't mean reconciliation with unsafe people, but it does mean reconciliation with yourself and with God. As long as you hold unforgiveness, your future is bound to your past. But when you forgive, you walk forward unchained, free to become all God created you to be. Forgiveness isn't weakness; it is your greatest strength. It is your declaration to hell itself that the cycle ends with you.

I remember the day I finally forgave my mother. It didn't happen at an altar call or in a big emotional moment. It happened one quiet morning in my prayer time when I told God how tired I was of feeling stuck. He whispered so clearly to my spirit, "Forgive her. She gave you what she had, but I give you what you need." I cried until my soul felt empty. But in that emptiness, God poured out His love. I began to see my mother as a broken little girl herself, repeating cycles that weren't hers to begin with. I didn't excuse what she did, but I chose to release it. That day, I unchained myself from the prison of being an abandoned little girl.

Forgiving my father was different. I always said I had nothing to forgive him for because he just wasn't there. But deep down, I was angry that he left me vulnerable. He left me uncovered and unprotected. He left me in the dark regarding a man's conversation, the gentle touch of a man who loves you with no ill intentions, and the safety of a loving father. I had to forgive him for the words he never spoke, the moments he never showed up for, and the protection he never gave. And when I did, a part of my heart came alive again.

Then there was me. Forgiving myself was the hardest part. Not just for the choices I've made, but for the shame I carried, the failures I replayed, and the silent judgments I held against my own heart. I had to stand in the mirror and speak grace over the girl staring back at me, a girl who has simply been trying to survive. She had inherited many strongholds, embraced false narratives, and, as a child, made decisions she was never equipped to make. That little girl didn't need more guilt; she needed compassion. I had to look her in the eyes and say, "You are forgiven. You are loved. You are redeemed. And in Christ Jesus, you are whole!" Only then did I begin to live like someone truly free.

I wish I could tell you that forgiving myself happened overnight. It didn't. It took time — years — to come to that sacred space of self-forgiveness and letting go. But healing isn't about speed; it's about surrender. It doesn't matter how long it takes. What matters is that you keep going, keep choosing freedom, one brave step at a time until your heart knows it's free ... truly free ... free indeed.

REFLECTION QUESTIONS

1. Who is one person in your life that you have struggled to forgive? What specific pain do you need to release to God today?
2. How has holding onto unforgiveness affected your emotional, spiritual, or physical health?
3. Do you believe that forgiveness means excusing what was done to you? How does God's definition of forgiveness differ from your own?
4. When you think about forgiving yourself, what emotions come up? Why do you think forgiving yourself has been so hard?
5. Write a prayer asking God to help you forgive — even if you don't feel ready — and to set you free from the chains of your past.
6. In what ways do you see unforgiveness keeping you chained to your past? How would your life be different if you chose forgiveness today?
7. Is there an area of your life where you are drinking "poison" and expecting someone else to be harmed? What step can you take today to release that toxic hold?
8. What does walking in forgiveness look like for you daily? How can you invite God into that process moment by moment?

RELEASING THE PAIN INTO GOD'S HANDS

1. Acknowledge the hurt. Write it out. Name what happened and how it impacted you.
2. Bring it to God. Ask Him to show you His perspective and what He wants to heal in you.
3. Choose to release. Speak it out loud: "I forgive ___ for ___. I release them and entrust them to God."

4. Pray blessings over them. This transforms your heart posture and uproots bitterness.
5. Forgive yourself. Accept God's grace and move forward in His freedom.
6. Repeat daily if needed. Forgiveness is a decision that often requires a process.

STATISTICS ON FORGIVENESS AND HEALING

*Studies show that forgiveness is associated with lower levels of depression, anxiety, and stress, and higher levels of self-esteem and life satisfaction (Toussaint, Worthington, & Williams, 2015).

*Forgiveness interventions have been linked to significant improvements in mental health outcomes, including reduced PTSD symptoms in trauma survivors (Lee & Enright, 2019).

PRAYER

Father God, thank You for Your unending mercy and forgiveness toward me I come before You with an open heart, asking You to help me release every chain of unforgiveness that has kept me bound. Lord, I confess that holding on to these hurts has only weighed me down and hindered my healing. I choose today to forgive those who have wounded me — not because they deserve it, but because You have forgiven me. Heal the broken places in my soul. Tear down every stronghold of bitterness, anger, resentment, pain. Pour out Your love and Your peace in every area where unforgiveness once lived. Teach me to walk in freedom, to extend grace as You have extended grace to me, and to live unchained from my past. In Jesus mighty name, Amen!

DECLARATION

I choose today to walk in the freedom of forgiveness. I release every person who has hurt me, intentionally or unintentionally. I forgive myself for my mistakes. I receive God's forgiveness and love. I will no longer be chained to the past. I am unchained, free, and whole in Jesus' name.

As God unchained me from the grip of unforgiveness, I realized something powerful: Healing is not just a decision; it is a journey. Forgiving those who hurt me broke the chains off my heart, but walking out my healing required intentional steps every single day. Forgiveness opened the prison door, but it was up to me to step out into freedom and begin living in the fullness God destined for me.

Now that you, too, have unlocked the power of forgiveness, it's time to put feet to your faith. It's time to walk it out — to take everything you've learned in these pages and apply it to your daily life. True healing isn't just about what happens in your private moments; it's about showing up to the world whole, free, and unbound.

MY SILENT REFLECTIONS

CHAPTER 12

Walk it Out: Your Guide to Healing

Scripture Focus:

Jeremiah 30:17 (NIV)

'But I will restore you to health and heal your wounds,' declares the Lord, 'because you are called an outcast, Zion for whom no one cares.'

Isaiah 58:8 (NIV)

Then your light will break forth like the dawn, and your healing will quickly appear; then your righteousness will go before you, and the glory of the Lord will be your rear guard.

Your healing is a weapon against the enemy's plan. Every step you take toward wholeness silences the lies he has spoken over your life.

You've journeyed with me through trauma, brokenness, secrets, abandonment, redemption, and deep inner healing. Now, my sister, it's time to walk it out.

Healing is not a one-time event. It is a daily choice to rise from the ashes of that which tried to bury you, and step boldly into who God created you to be. As you stand here at the edge of everything you've survived, I want you to hear me clearly:

You were never meant to just survive — you were created to thrive.

Part of walking this journey out is giving yourself grace and space. Healing doesn't thrive in the soil of shame or self-condemnation. It grows when you allow yourself to breathe, rest, and release the pressure of having it all together. Grace means understanding that setbacks don't erase your progress. Space means creating room for God to move in your heart, to surround you with safe community, and to carry you when you can't carry yourself. This journey is not one you can take alone, but the good news is you don't have to — because the God who goes before you has promised to never leave you or forsake you (Deuteronomy 31:6, Hebrews 13:5). He walks every step beside you.

Healing is not passive; it's intentional. It is waking up each day and declaring, "I will not be defined by my past, my pain, or my mistakes. I am defined by God's truth, His love, and His purpose for my life." This chapter is your blueprint. It is where tears turn into prayers, where prayers turn into strategies, and where strategies turn into powerful action. Healing is a daily decision to show up for yourself with God leading the way. As you close this book, I want you to take these next steps with courage, intention, and fierce faith. Because healing isn't just for you. It's for every life connected to yours.

There comes a moment when the pain stops defining you and starts refining you. When you finally let go of the bitterness, the unforgiveness, and the shame, something shifts.

The very wounds that tried to silence me became the voice God uses to help heal others. I've learned that pain, surrendered to God, becomes a platform for purpose. Through healing and forgiveness, I found hope again. Not the kind you fake to get through the day, but the kind that anchors your soul and reminds you that beauty truly can rise from ashes. This is the power of redemption. This is the miracle of healing.

Many people cling to the saying that "time heals all wounds," but it's a comforting lie rather than the raw truth. Time alone does not erase pain, guilt, betrayal, or grief — it only allows wounds to fester under the surface if left untreated. As a nursing professional, I've done my share of wound care, and the one thing I know for sure is this: for most wounds I treated, what they needed most was exposure. A wound that stays covered up never truly heals; it festers beneath the surface oftentimes. The wound may appear closed on the surface but is infected from within. Healing requires air, light, offloading of pressure, and sometimes even discomfort. The same is for the soul. What doesn't get exposed will never heal. Just like an untreated wound on the skin, an unhealed wound in the soul can become infected. It may look fine on the surface, but beneath that false covering lies pain, bitterness, and decay. That untreated infection in the soul spreads to our relationships, our self-worth, and even our faith. What festers in us silently begins to poison the beauty God intended to flow from us. True healing comes from the Great Physician, who mends the brokenhearted, restores what was lost, and gives peace that surpasses understanding. Only He can transform deep hurts into strength, forgiveness, and redemption. While time may soften edges or dull memories, it is God who truly heals, renewing hearts and souls in ways that nothing else — even the passage of years — can accomplish.

Healing is not the final destination where you arrive and declare yourself "finished." Healing is a lifelong journey — sometimes slow, sometimes surprising, but always worth it. Along the way, there will be days when you feel strong and whole, and other days when old wounds resurface. That doesn't mean you've failed — it means you're human. Healing is about allowing God to meet you right where you are, moment by moment, layer by layer, transforming your pain into purpose. It's about walking with Him daily and letting His love write a new story over your life.

Healing isn't a destination – it's a daily decision to rise, walk and become who God destined you to be. Your healing, your freedom, your destiny — they are waiting for you to take the first step.

WALK OUT YOUR HEALING

1. Acknowledge Your Reality.
   You cannot heal what you refuse to confront. Name your pain, your fears, your regrets, and your shame. Bring them to the light.
2. Invite God In.
   Healing without God is behavior modification. Healing with God is soul transformation. Remember, God specializes in the messy, broken places in our lives.
3. Seek Professional Help if Needed.
   Therapy, counseling, and pastoral care are gifts from God. They do not replace your faith — they partner with it to set you free.
4. Forgive.
   Forgiveness is not approval of what happened; it is releasing yourself from the bondage it created. Ask God to help you forgive others — and yourself.
5. Speak Life Daily.
   Replace trauma's lies with God's truth. I am loved. I am chosen. I am redeemed. I am enough. (Psalm 139:14)
6. Protect Your Gates.
   Watch what you allow into your mind and spirit — music, movies, conversations, social media. Your freedom is too precious to compromise.
7. Connect With a Faith Community.
   You were never meant to heal alone. Surround yourself with **mature** believers who will cover you in prayer, speak truth over you, and walk alongside you.

8. Prioritize Self-Care.
Rest. Eat well. Move your body. Laugh. Journal. Worship. Healing is holistic.
9. Remember Your Why.
Your healing is not just for you. It's for your children, your spouse, your family, your ministry, your community, and every woman watching your life to see if freedom is truly possible.
10. Keep Going.
Healing is a journey, not a destination. There will be days you feel stuck. Don't stop. Get back up and walk it out.

POWERFUL STATISTICS

- Nearly 70% of adults in the U.S. have experienced some type of traumatic event at least once in their lives (National Council for Mental Wellbeing, 2021).
- Women who engage in consistent trauma-informed therapy experience a 32% greater improvement in emotional health outcomes (SAMHSA, 2014b).
- Less than 50% of African American women who experience depression or trauma-related symptoms receive adequate mental health care (Ward & Heidrich, 2009).

Your healing journey is not just spiritual; it is strategic. Seek the help God provides.

REFLECTION QUESTIONS

1. What areas of your life have you avoided bringing into the light? (Psalm 139:23-24)
2. How am I trusting God with the parts of my healing that I don't yet understand? (Proverbs 3:5-6)

3. Are my thoughts helping or hindering my healing? What truths from God's word can I focus on to renew my mind and strengthen my spirit (Romans 12:2)
4. Who is your safe faith community that will walk this out with you? (Hebrews 10:24-25)
5. What is one daily habit you will begin today to prioritize your healing? (Joshua 1:9)
6. When I stumble or feel discouraged in my healing journey, what steps can I take to keep moving forward and not give up? How do I celebrate small victories along the way? (Galatians 6:9)

PRAYER

Heavenly Father, thank You for walking with me through every dark valley and broken place in my life. Thank You for revealing truth, for uncovering hidden wounds, and calling me into freedom. I ask for Your strength and courage as I step forward in my healing journey. Help me not to just hear Your word, but to walk it out daily with a bold faith and unwavering trust. Let Your Holy Spirit guide my steps and keep me anchored in Your love. May I become a living testimony of Your healing power and redeeming grace. Teach me to love myself the way You love me; to honor the story You've written for my life, and to extend Your healing to others around me. I declare that I will rise, I will overcome, and I will walk in the fullness of purpose and freedom You have ordained for me. In Jesus' powerful name, Amen.

DECLARATION

I declare that I am walking out of the shadows and into God's marvelous light (1 Peter 2:9). I will no longer bow to the lies of trauma or the residue of my past. I am redeemed. I am restored. I am whole. My healing is my testimony, and my life is a weapon in the hand of God. From this day forward, I walk in purpose, on purpose, for His glory alone. I am free, and I will stay free.

Final Charge

Your story matters deeply. None of your pain has been wasted. God is weaving it into purpose. Healing is your portion — a divine gift from your Heavenly Father. You have an Advocate who fights for you and walks beside you every step of the way. Remember, your healing is not just for you; it is a gift to the world. So, rise up, strong woman, and walk it out! The world is waiting for your freedom story to unlock theirs!

MY SILENT REFLECTIONS

CLOSING WORD

As you close the pages of this book, I want you to pause and take a deep breath. Let truth wash over you. **You are not the woman you were when you began reading Chapter One.** You are not defined by your pain, trauma, or silent cries. You are defined by the One who created you with intentionality, who formed you in your mother's womb, who called you by name, and who has declared that you are fearfully and wonderfully made.

Today I speak life over you:

You are healed. You are whole.

You are free. You are chosen, cherished, and deeply loved; you are no longer a prisoner of your past.

You are no longer bound by the lies that trauma told you. You are no longer hidden in the shadows of shame.

You are the radiant daughter of the Most High God, crowned with dignity, clothed with strength, walking boldly in purpose and in power.

I declare that, from this day forward, you will rise in the authority of your identity in Christ. You will silence every voice that says you are not enough. You will stand firm against every generational curse that has tried to follow you. You will walk in your healing daily, choosing to love yourself with the love that your Heavenly Father lavishes upon you.

I speak courage over you to do the work of healing, to reach back and rescue the little girl within you, to embrace forgiveness, and to walk unchained into your divine future. May the oil of joy replace your mourning, and may a garment of praise clothe every place where heaviness once lived.

You are unstoppable, unbreakable, and unshakable in Him.

Rise, daughter, and sound the alarm of your freedom. The world is waiting for your story, your voice, and your victory.

Now go forth. Walk it out. Live it out loud. You are a strong woman whose silent cries have become a roaring anthem of God's glory.

REFERENCES

American Psychological Association. (2019). Marriage and divorce. https://www.apa.org

Centers for Disease Control and Prevention. (2021). Adverse Childhood Experiences (ACEs). https://www.cdc.gov/violenceprevention/aces/index.html

Centers for Disease Control and Prevention. (2023). Childhood trauma and adult health outcomes. https://www.cdc.gov/violenceprevention/aces/fastfact.html

Child Trends. (2019). Parenting practices and child well-being. https://www.childtrends.org/indicators/parental-involvement-in-schools

Felitti, V. J., Anda, R. F., Nordenberg, D., Williamson, D. F., Spitz, A. M., Edwards, V., ... & Marks, J. S. (1998). Relationship of childhood abuse and household dysfunction to many of the leading causes of death in adults: The Adverse Childhood Experiences (ACE) study. American Journal of Preventive Medicine, 14(4), 245–258. https://doi.org/10.1016/S0749-3797(98)00017-8

Johnson, S. M. (2004). The practice of emotionally focused couple therapy: Creating connection. Brunner-Routledge.

Lee, Y. R., & Enright, R. D. (2019). A meta-analysis of the association between forgiveness of others and physical health. Psychology & Health, 34(5), 626–643.

National Child Traumatic Stress Network. (n.d.). About child trauma. https://www.nctsn.org/what-is-child-trauma/about-child-trauma

National Council for Mental Wellbeing. (2021). Trauma-informed care: An overview. https://www.thenationalcouncil.org

National Eating Disorders Association. (2022). Statistics & research on eating disorders. https://www.nationaleatingdisorders.org/statistics-research-eating-disorders

Reddy, M. K., et al. (2014). The impact of partner support on psychological distress among trauma survivors. Journal of Interpersonal Violence, 29(14), 2757–2776.

Substance Abuse and Mental Health Services Administration. (2014). SAMHSA's concept of trauma and guidance for a trauma-informed approach (HHS Publication No. SMA14-4884). https://ncsacw.samhsa.gov/userfiles/files/SAMHSA_Trauma.pdf

Substance Abuse and Mental Health Services Administration. (2014). Trauma-informed care in behavioral health services (Treatment Improvement Protocol Series 57).

Toussaint, L., Worthington, E. L., & Williams, D. R. (2015). Forgiveness and health: Scientific evidence and theories relating forgiveness to better health. Springer.

Udo, T., & Grilo, C. M. (2018). Prevalence and correlates of DSM-5–defined eating disorders in a nationally representative sample of U.S. adults. Biological Psychiatry, 84(5), 345–354. https://doi.org/10.1016/j.biopsych.2018.03.014

U.S. Census Bureau. (2020). Living arrangements of children under 18 years old: 1960 to present. https://www.census.gov

Van Strien, T., & Ouwens, M. A. (2007). Effects of distress, alexithymia and impulsivity on eating. Eating Behaviors, 8(2), 251–257. https://doi.org/10.1016/j.eatbeh.2006.06.004

Ward, E. C., & Heidrich, S. (2009). African American women's beliefs about mental illness, stigma, and preferred coping behaviors. Research in Nursing & Health, 32(5), 480–492.

www.ingramcontent.com/pod-product-compliance
Lightning Source LLC
LaVergne TN
LVHW020647100826
845148LV00012B/2368